Bond of Secrecy

My Life with CIA Spy and Watergate Conspirator E. Howard Hunt

Saint John Hunt

Startling new information about Watergate and the JFK assassination, including hand-written memos from E. Howard Hunt's famous "final confession."

Published by:
Trine Day LLC
PO Box 577
Walterville, OR 97489
1-800-556-2012
www.TrineDay.com
publisher@trineday.net

Library of Congress Control Number: 2012949731

Hunt, Saint John.
Bonds of Secrecy - My Life with CIA Spy and Watergate Conspirator
E. Howard Hunt—1st ed.
p. cm.
Epub (ISBN-13) 978-1-936296-84-2 (ISBN-10) 1-936296-84-5
Kindle (ISBN-13) 978-1-936296-85-9 (ISBN-10) 1-936296-85-3
Print (ISBN-13) 978-1-936296-83-5 (ISBN-10) 1-936296-83-7
1. Hunt, E. Howard (Everette Howard) 1918-2007. 2. Kennedy, John F.
(John Fitzgerald) 1917-1963—Assassination. 3. Watergate Affair, 1972-
1974. 4. Intelligence services—United States—History—20th century. 5.
United States—Politics and government, 1945-1989. I. Title

First Edition
10 9 8 7 6 5 4 3 2

Printed in the USA
Distribution to the Trade by:
Independent Publishers Group (IPG)
814 North Franklin Street
Chicago, Illinois 60610
312.337.0747
www.ipgbook.com

For Dorothy

Is there an answer that makes it okay
For God or the Devil to take you away
You gave birth to me, a reason to be
I still am your son, but your life is done

Is there a meaning, what is the gain?
That makes it worth living with all of this pain
I won't let you go, I want you to know
My love will survive, but you're not alive

I miss you

FOREWORD

*The great enemy of truth is very often not the lie – deliber-
ate, contrived and dishonest – but the myth – persistent,
persuasive, and unrealistic. Too often ... we enjoy the com-
fort of opinion without the discomfort of thought.*

–President John F. Kennedy, Commencement Address at Yale University,
Old Campus, New Haven, Connecticut, June 11, 1962

By Jesse Ventura

Stated simply, "Something stinks."

I wish we knew the truth about the murder of JFK.

Maybe we do, but the corporate media repeatedly shouts at us that we don't. Always laying the blame squarely on the shoulders of lone nut Lee Oswald ... yet nothing has been proved and no one has ever been punished.

Regardless of what the "official" findings may say, after near fifty years the mystery remains unsolved. What a tribute to the power of those who pulled off the greatest crime of the 20th century.

To make our task even harder, the keepers of the secrets first said that seventy-five years (2038) must pass before we, the people, can be trusted with many of the hard facts about this terrible event – when those who lived through it are dead.

After Oliver Stone's film, *JFK*, came out in 1991, the public outcry resulted in the creation of the Assassination Records Review Board (AARB), which was given the job of releasing all of the withheld documents. But, according to a 2012 letter from the Assassination Archives and Research Center there are approximately 50,000 documents still held as classified, and unavailable for public review.

Let me add my voice to those who call for the release of all of these documents. Without all the information what's left is a smelly puzzle with many of the most important pieces missing – plus some extra pieces thrown in ... to "play" with us.

From the citizen-demanded AARB document releases, we learned about Operations Northwoods, a proposal by the Department of Defense and the Joint Chiefs of Staff for President Kennedy to use the CIA to mount false-flag operations against Cuba. Aircraft disguised as Cuban planes were to attack American targets. JFK nixed the illegal action.

Some say that President Kennedy's unwillingness to do the bidding of our national security state led to his murder. Others say it was a Mafia hit, and then the state's secret squads hushed it up because their association with the Mafia compromised them. And there are so many other tales, including several variations of officialdom's "Oswald did it" refrain. You listen and look long enough, and you soon find out why "conspiracy theory" gets such a bad rap. There is just so much hogwash, hooey and hokum out there.

With St. John Hunt's book, *Bond of Secrecy*, we get to hear from someone who was involved in the horrid crime, CIA spy and Watergate burglar, E. Howard Hunt. There is interesting courtroom testimony that Hunt was involved in one of the assassination's many threads: as Eduardó, the paymaster for the CIA's exiled Cuban "franchise." And before his death, after being thwarted in the telling of his tale, he arranged to give his oldest son the story of his involvement.

Hunt was no Johnny-come-lately to deep politics, he had been involved in the netherworld of espionage since World War II, and was present at many of our country's secrets. He had been with OSS in China, a CIA station chief in Mexico City in the 1950s, part of the Guatemala project in 1954, and he served as the first Chief of Covert Action for the CIA's Domestic Operations Division.

While I can say that these will not be the last words on the JFK assassination, these are the last words and thoughts of a man who said he had been approached to be on the game-day hit-team. He declined, but accepted a role as "benchwarmer." From that position, Hunt had quite the view.

Can we trust what Hunt tells his son here any better than what he has said before? After his public exposure during Watergate Hunt became embroiled within various different conspiracy theories, and had numerous governmental investigation and court appearances about the JFK assassination. He has told several different versions of his involvement: a story about a boy and a wolf comes to mind. So, we cannot know for certain, but we can use what Hunt tell us to explore and hopefully understand those ingrained events of November 22, 1963.

Hunt points us towards exiled Cubans, disgruntled CIA officers and LBJ. Others also finger the same crew, and I have no doubt that they were involved. But, there had to be others, and we need to have our government obey the law, and release all the JFK related documents now, not later.

I want my country back; we need transparency from our elected officials, not cover-up. But I won't hold my breath.

Until we get truth from our government we must find it where we can. St. John Hunt's book, *Bond of Secrecy* is one place. We can gather insight from its amazing story of the first-born son in the family of a very notorious spy, where truth may be fleeting but also very profound.

Jesse Ventura
October 12, 2012

INTRODUCTION

By Douglas Caddy
Original Attorney for the Watergate Seven

BEFORE WATERGATE

When I first met Howard Hunt in 1970, my immediate impression was of a man who was highly intelligent, possessed perfect manners and was extremely articulate in his conversation.

The occasion of our first meeting was Howard's coming on board as an employee at the Robert Mullen & Company upon his "retiring" from the CIA. The Mullen Company was a public relations firm with its headquarters in Washington, D.C. and with offices scattered around the globe. General Foods Corporation was a Mullen Company account. I had gone to work for General Foods in White Plains, New York, not long after graduating in 1966 from the New York University Law School. In 1969 General Foods assigned me to work out of the Mullen Company in conjunction with my job representing General Foods' interests in the nation's capital.

Howard and I quickly became friends once we learned that we had another friend in common: William F. Buckley, Jr., publisher of *National Review* magazine. I had worked closely with Buckley in the founding of the modern conservative movement in the late 1950s and early 1960s. I had served as the first National Director of Young Americans for Freedom, a nationwide youth organization, which had been founded in September 1960 at a gathering of young conservative activists at the Buckley family compound in Sharon, Connecticut.

From Howard I learned something that I did not know: that Buckley at one time had been a CIA agent and had worked under Howard's supervision in Mexico City for a year after graduating from Yale University, where he had been selected for Skull & Bones.

As our friendship burgeoned, neither Howard nor I had any prescient inkling that two years later he would become a central figure in a scandal that would change the course of history and of my life and career.

A few months after our initial meeting, Robert Mullen called us into his office and surprised us by saying that he desired to retire and wanted to sell the Mullen Company. He then asked if we would be interested in purchasing it. He proposed that the sale would be financed over the ensuing years by payments to him of profits from the company's public relations accounts, which included General Foods, the Mormon Church, a lucrative federal government contract with the Department of Health and Human Services and several others.

Both Howard and I were stunned by Mullen's proposal and told him that we needed time to consider it. Mullen agreed and during the next two months we had additional meetings with him about the purchase. However, at these subsequent meetings Mullen seemed to forget key details that we had discussed previously about the purchase, causing Howard several times to query me about whether I thought Mullen was suffering from the onset of dementia.

Then one day Mullen announced out of the blue that he had decided to sell his company to Robert Bennett, a Mormon who was the son of the senior U.S. Senator from Utah. What I came to learn years later was that Mullen, Bennett and Hunt knew something that had been kept from me, namely that the Mullen Company had been incorporated by the CIA in 1959 and served as a front for the intelligence agency. The Mullen Company offices around the world were in fact operations of the CIA, and General Foods was aware of this and a participant in the overall intelligence scheme. Although Hunt was a protégé of CIA Director Richard Helms and had been placed by Helms inside the Mullen Company, a decision had been made by the CIA that one of its other key operatives, Robert

Bennett, would purchase the Mullen Company and become its president.

After meeting Bennett and finding him to be an extremely strange man who exuded duplicity I chose to leave General Foods and went to work as an attorney with the Washington law firm of Gall, Lane, Powell and Kilcullen. Howard stayed with the Mullen Company as its vice president.

Soon after I began work at the law firm, Howard contacted me and asked that I perform legal work for him. I readily agreed and did so along with one of the partners of the law firm, Robert Scott, who found Howard to be an intriguing client.

In mid-1971 Howard informed me that he was under consideration to work in the White House while still an employee of the Mullen Company. His sponsor for the position was Charles Colson, one of President Nixon's closest aides and an alumnus, like Howard, of Brown University. Howard asked if I would write a letter of recommendation for his appointment, which I promptly did.

Once Howard began working for the White House, we saw each other only intermittently. However, on several occasions he invited me to join him and his colleague, Gordon Liddy, for lunch at the Federal City Club. Both men were circumspect in their discussion in my presence, but from what I gathered they were involved in hush-hush, sensitive work on behalf of the White House.

In February 1972, John Killcullen, one of the partners of the law firm that employed me, informed me that I was being assigned to do volunteer work for the Lawyers Committee for the Re-Election of the President. I soon met with John Dean, Counsel to the President, in his White House office and he in turn, after explaining the campaign legal work I would be doing, assigned me to work with one of his assistants, another lawyer.

Howard was delighted to learn of my newly assigned task and so was Gordon Liddy, who at one point asked me to do legal research for him and the Finance Committee for the

Re-Election of the President. The head of the Finance Committee was Maurice Stans, a close friend of Nixon.

In April 1972 Howard asked me to join him and the General Counsel for the CIA, Lawrence Huston, at a restaurant in Maryland, not far from the CIA headquarters on the other side of the Potomac River. At the meeting the two men sounded me out as to whether I would be interested in going to work for the CIA. If I were agreeable, my assignment would be to move to Nicaragua and there build and manage a luxurious seaside hotel that would lure the Sandinista leaders. This would allow the CIA to learn more about them. I told Howard and Huston I would think about it, but for certain reasons decided immediately I would not accept their job offer.

Two months later Watergate broke with the arrests of the five burglars inside the offices of the Democratic National Committee.

During Watergate

The narrative is picked up in a passage from Howard Hunt's 1974 book, *Undercover: Memoirs of an American Secret Agent*:

> "I drove to the White House Annex – the Old Executive Office Building, in bygone years the War Department and later the Department of State.
>
> "Carrying three heavy attaché cases, I entered the Pennsylvania Avenue door, showed my blue-and-white White House pass to the uniformed guards, and took the elevator to the third floor. I unlocked the door of 338 and went in. I opened my two-drawer safe, took out my operational handbook, found a telephone number and dialed it.
>
> "The time was 3:13 in the morning of June 17, 1972, and five of my companions had been arrested and taken to the maximum-security block of the District of Columbia jail. I had recruited four of them and it was my responsibility to get them out. That was the sole focus of my thoughts as I began talking on the telephone.

"But with those five arrests the Watergate affair had begun ...

"After several rings the call was answered and I heard the sleepy voice of Douglas Caddy.

"'Yes?'

"'Doug? This is Howard. I hate to wake you up, but I've got a tough situation and I need to talk to you. Can I come over?'

"'Sure. I'll tell the desk clerk you're expected.'

"'I'll be there in about 20 minutes,' I told him, and hung up.

"From the safe I took a small money box and removed the $10,000 Liddy had given me for emergency use. I put $1,500 in my wallet and the remaining $8,500 in my coat pocket. The black attaché case containing McCord's electronic equipment I placed in a safe drawer that held my operational notebook. Then I closed and locked the safe, turning the dial several times. The other two cases I left beside the safe, turned out the light and left my office, locking the door."

About half an hour after he telephoned me, Hunt arrived at my Washington apartment located in the Georgetown House at 2121 P St., N.W., about a five-minute drive from the both the Watergate and the White House. He quickly informed me of what had occurred.

Hunt then telephoned Liddy from my apartment and they both requested that I represent them as their attorney in the case as well as the five arrested individuals – James McCord and the four Cuban-Americans.

On June 28 – 11 days later – I was served with a subpoena to appear "Forthwith" before the grand jury. The subpoena was served on me by Assistant U.S. Attorney Donald Campbell while I was in the federal court house. He grabbed me by my arm and pulled me into the grand jury room.

The prosecutors asked me hundred of questions over the next two weeks and subpoenaed my personal bank records. Ultimately I refused to answer 38 questions that I and the five attorneys representing me believed were protected by the attorney-client privilege. For example, one question was: "At what time did you receive a telephone call in the early morning hours of June 17, 1972?" By answering this question, I could ultimately be forced to identify Hunt and thus incriminate him.

Principal Assistant U.S. Attorney Earl Silbert argued in court that my refusal to answer the grand jury questions on the grounds of the attorney-client privilege was "specious, dilatory and ... an obstruction of justice."

Judge John Sirica, who had assigned himself to try the Watergate case, saw a golden opportunity to inflate his towering ego and exercise his unlimited ambition at the expense of justice and the country. At a hearing on July 12, 1972 – less than a month after the case broke – Sirica rejected outright my attorneys' argument that the attorney-client privilege was being egregiously violated by the 38 questions. Declared Sirica to a courtroom packed with lawyers, the press and spectators:

"You see, to put the matter perfectly bluntly, if the government is trying to get enough evidence to indict Mr. Caddy as one of the principals in this case even though he might not have been present at the time of the alleged entry in this place, I don't know what the evidence is except what has been disclosed here. If the government is trying to get an indictment against Mr. Caddy and he feels that way and you feel it and the rest of you attorneys feel it, all he has to say is 'I refuse to answer on the grounds what I say would tend to incriminate me.' That ends it. I can't compel him to say he knows Mr. Hunt under the circumstances. He doesn't do that, understand? He takes the other road. He says there is a confidential communication. Who is he to be the sole judge of what is confidential or not? That is what I am here for."

The next day, after I refused to answer the 38 questions before the grand jury on the grounds that doing so would violate the attorney-client privilege, Sirica convened a court hearing to hold me in contempt.

Robert Scott, one of my attorneys who later was named a District of Columbia judge, asked Sirica to honor professional courtesy by not ordering me jailed while an appeal was filed with the U.S. Court of Appeals for the District of Columbia Circuit, stating:

"If Your Honor please, there is nothing malicious in this refusal. It is done in good faith, good conscience, it is done because we believe it is the proper course. I would respectfully suggest this is very harsh treatment – not the finding of contempt, I don't say that. I disagree that he should be found in contempt, but I think it is very harsh treatment that your honor would commit him when it is perfectly clear that these positions are being put forth in the utmost good faith and utmost of sincerity. This is a young man, I just think it would be as harsh as it could be to commit him at this time."

Of course, this plea fell upon the deaf ears of a judicial bully and thug who took delight in destroying the careers and lives and the innocent as well as the guilty. Sirica ordered the U.S. Marshal to take me into custody to be jailed.

On July 18, 1972 the U.S. Court of Appeals affirmed Sirica's contempt citation of me. It did so in by employing gratuitously insulting language, declaring, "Even if such a relationship does exist, certain communications, such as in furtherance of a crime, are not within the [attorney-client] privilege."

The day after the decision of the Court of Appeals, I appeared again before the grand jury and pursuant to the threat posed by the Court's decision answered all the questions posed to me by the prosecutors.

The actions of Sirica and the Court of Appeals did not go unnoticed by the White House. In an Oval Office tape of July 19, 1972, an incredulous President Nixon asked John Ehrlichman, "Do you mean the circuit court ordered an attorney to testify?" to which Ehrlichman responded, "It [unintelligible] to me, except that this damn circuit we've got here with [Judge David] Bazelon and so on, it surprises me every time they do something."

Nixon then asked, "Why didn't he appeal to the Supreme Court?"

What Nixon and Ehrlichman did not realize was that I and my attorneys firmly believed that we had created a strong legal record that the constitutional rights of the defendants and me as their attorney had been egregiously violated. If Hunt, Liddy and the five arrested defendants were found guilty, their convictions could then be overturned as a result of the abusive actions of the prosecutors, Judge Sirica and the Court of Appeals.

However, Sirica's vitriolic courtroom antics, aided and abetted by a biased Court of Appeals, had the effect of encouraging the defendants to embark on a "hush money" cover-up after they realized early on that the courts were not going to give them a fair trial. Hunt later wrote that "If Sirica was treating Caddy – an Officer of the Court – so summarily, and Caddy was completely uninvolved in Watergate – then those of us who were involved could expect neither fairness nor understanding from him. As events unfolded, this conclusion became tragically accurate." Bear in mind all the above described courtroom events occurred in the first 33 days of the case. The dye has been cast by the prosecutors and the judges to deny the seven defendants a fair trial.

Shortly after indictments were handed down against all seven defendants in September 1972, the prosecutors informed me that I would be a government witness at their trial and that I should review my grand jury transcripts in their office in preparation of so testifying.

William Bittman, a former Justice Department prosecutor who succeeded me in representing Hunt, advised me that because the prosecutors had gone too far in their persecution of me, they had jeopardized their case and were worried about that fact. No evidence had been uncovered over the months since the case broke that I had engaged in any criminal activity. One of the prosecutors even disclosed that an examination of my personal bank records, obtained by subpoena, revealed that I was "scrupulously honest." Bittman then instructed me that when I reviewed my grand jury transcripts I should diligently determine if any alterations had been made in them. His fear was that the prosecutors had rewritten my testimony so as to weaken the attorney-client privilege. He said that if I found any of my transcripts had been altered, he planned to call Silbert to the witness stand at the trial to question him about the alteration. He declared, "Hunt deserves a fair trial and I am going to see that he gets one."

When I did review the grand jury transcripts, I determined that a key alteration had been made by the prosecutors. This alteration dealt with my attempt to tell the grand jury on July 19, 1972, that I had been approached in early July to act as conduit for "hush money" to be distributed to the defendants.

The overture was made by Anthony Ulasewicz, a former New York City police detective, acting upon the instructions of Herbert Kalmbach, President Nixon's personal attorney. Here is the testimony of Kalmbach subsequently before the Senate Watergate Committee:

"Mr. Dash: Now, what was the first instruction you received to give the money?

"Mr. Kalmbach: Again, as I have tried to reconstruct this, Mr. Dash, the first instruction that I received, which I passed to Mr. Ulasewicz was to have Mr. Ulasewicz give $25,000 to Mr. Caddy. I don't know too much of Mr. Caddy, I understand that he is an attorney here in Washington. And, as I recall it, this was probably from approximately July 1 through July 6 or 7. There were a number of calls. I would either talk to Mr. Dean or Mr. LaRue. I would then call Mr. Ulasewicz who, in turn, would call Mr. Caddy. He would have some response from Mr. Caddy, and I would call back up either Mr. Dean or Mr. LaRue.

"Mr. Dash: What was the response from Mr. Caddy?

"Mr. Kalmbach: Well, the sum and gist of it was that Mr. Caddy refused to accept the funds.

"Mr. Dash: In that manner?

"Mr. Kalmbach: That is correct. That was the end-all. There were several phone calls, but the final wrap-up won it was that he refused the funds."

My grand jury testimony was not the only one altered by the prosecutors. Alfred Baldwin, a key figure in the case, later charged that his grand jury testimony also had been altered by the prosecutors.

At the first Watergate trial, Hunt and the four Cuban-Americans pleaded guilty at its beginning. This came about because about a month previously Dorothy Hunt had died in a mysterious plane crash in Chicago. For Hunt, a trial following on the heels of his wife's tragic death was more than he could bear. The four Cuban-Americans, loyal to a fault to Hunt, followed his lead. Liddy and McCord stood trial and were found guilty.

Liddy appealed his conviction. The same Court of Appeals that had forced me to testify before the grand jury in its gratuitously insulting decision opined as to the defendant Liddy being denied Sixth Amendment counsel because of what the courts had done to me as his attorney: "The evidence against appellant ... was so overwhelming that even if there were constitutional error in the comment of the prosecutor and the instruction of the judge, there is no reasonable possibility it contributed to the conviction."

Of course, neither Judge Sirica, whom *Time* magazine later named "Man Of The Year," nor the U.S. Court of Appeals ever acknowledged that their abusive actions and decisions in the first month of the case relating to me and the attorney-client privilege were a principal cause of the cover-up that ensued.

Sirica later wrote a book about Watergate, fatuously titled *To Set the Record Straight*, for which he pocketed one million dollars, which would be almost four million of today's dollars. James Jackson Kilpatrick, a nationally syndicated columnist, wrote at the time: "It would be pleasant if someone would set the record straight about this tin pot tyrant. Sirica is a vainglorious pooh-bah.... When the Watergate criminal trials were assigned to him in the fall of 1972, he set out to enjoin the whole countryside with an encompassing gag order that perfectly reflected his lust for power. The order was patently absurd – it embraced even 'potential witnesses' and 'alleged victims' and had to be watered down."

Despite the efforts of the prosecutors, Sirica and the Court of Appeals to set me up, I was never indicted, named as an unindicted co-conspirator, disciplined by the Bar or even contacted by the Senate Watergate Committee.

Watergate, as Senator Sam Ervin, Chairman of the Senate Watergate Committee said at the time, was the most publicized event in American political history. It certainly was the country's biggest criminal case of the 20th century.

POST WATERGATE

I believe the media has painted an erroneous portrait of who Howard actually was. A fuller picture of the man is shown in the 2012 book *Watergate: The Hidden History* by Lamar Waldron, which contains numerous references to Howard and his career. Waldron writes, "Some writers depict Hunt as a minor figure, bumbling his way from one small White House operation to the next. However, a review of all the evidence shows that Hunt was consistently working on important tasks for the White House, on matters that interested the President. Hunt also kept expanding (or wanting to expand) his operations, which often overlapped with other projects that he sought out or pushed. The more Nixon operations Hunt became involved in, the higher his status in the White House and the better for his future. It was also good for his mentor, Richard Helms, since it gave him access to the White House (and FBI) information and operations. The President's White House staff was expanding its illegal operations on his behalf so rapidly that Hunt had no problem finding Nixon aides who wanted Hunt's services, to help them achieve the illicit goals the President wanted. That symbiotic relationship would soon grow so rapidly that it would start to spiral out of control, with disastrous results for all concerned."

As I look back I have come to the conclusion that the CIA had a goal of placing Howard in the White House in 1971, and that he thought of himself more as a CIA agent than as a trusted member of the White House staff. Thus, after the Watergate "hush" money scheme was exposed, Howard was quoted in *People* magazine of May 20, 1974: "I had always assumed, working for the CIA for so many years, that anything the White House wanted done was the law of the land. I viewed this like any other mission. It just happened to take place inside this country."

Howard's longtime friend and former CIA colleague William F. Buckley, Jr. accurately assessed him as follows: "Hunt had lived outside the law in the service of his country, subsequently of President Nixon ... Hunt, the dramatist, didn't understand the political realities at the highest level transcend the working realities of spy life."

While Howard revealed a lack of political awareness during Watergate, on another important political topic he was right on target. As the *New York Post* reported on January 14, 2007, he originally wrote in his memoir, *American Spy: My Secret History in the CIA, Watergate and Beyond*, published in 2007, that "Having Kennedy liquidated, thus elevating himself to the presidency without having to work for it himself, could have been a very tempting and logical move on [Lyndon] Johnson's part.

"LBJ had the money and the connections to manipulate the scenario in Dallas and is on record as having convinced JFK to make the appearance in the first place. He further tried unsuccessfully to engineer the passengers in each vehicle, trying to get his good buddy, Governor [John] Connally, to ride with him instead of JFK's car – where ... he would have been out of danger"

Howard pinpointed CIA agent William Harvey as playing a key role in the JFK assassination: "He definitely had dreams of becoming [CIA director] and LBJ could do that for him if he were president. [LBJ] would have used Harvey because he was available and corrupt."

Just prior the memoir's publication, passages that dealt with advance knowledge possessed by Howard of JFK's assassination were removed at the insistence of Howard's then lawyer. However, Howard, ever the consummate intelligence officer, clandestinely arranged that his views on Kennedy's murder would ultimately be publicly made known by giving his son, St. John, an audio tape to be released after his death in which he described the planning of the assassination. This is why St. John Hunt's book is an important contribution to history.

Douglas Caddy
September, 22, 2012

CONTENTS

1957, Tokyo Japan. Papa's ears would be surgically altered shortly after 1963. L-R, Dorothy, St. John, Lisa, E. Howard and Kevan

Chapter One

WATERGATE IN CONTEXT

I've always thought of myself as being of sound moral character. As I move through my fifties, I feel this statement is substantiated by the fact that, though I have pushed the envelope of legality, never once have I been accused of double dealing or other unethical behavior. As with all self-assessments, these value judgments can be different from the ones other people may have. Everyone likes to think they're honest and true, but there are always others who have a different agenda or whose story comes into conflict with your own. Having said that, and realizing full well that at least the members of my family may object to the story I'm about to relate, I will recount events in my life that have had a profound effect on me. After wrestling with many of the issues that arise out of this story, I've reached a simple ideology: you can't make everybody happy all the time.

Another factor that has weighed heavily on my mind is the concept of truth, one of those lofty principles that most of us try to keep in our embrace. However, we all know that when truth hurts, it's easier to turn away. But what if avoiding truth creates a deeper hurt? I guess you'd have to consider whom you're hurting, and what the stakes are in telling that truth. People say, "There's only one truth." I find that a questionable supposition. Certainly, if you tell a lie, you aren't telling the truth. But consider truth as a three-dimensional value. Truth would then be subject to point of view.

What I see and therefore "know," might be different from what the person on the other side of this three-dimensional value sees, and therefore knows. This variance, then, brings into play moral and ethical issues. People "see" things in a way that supports the agenda that they have. The agenda I have in writing this story is to recount, to the best of my recollection, only those events of which I have direct knowledge and involvement.

As is true in many families, the children of my parents (there are four) fulfilled many of the standard, stereotypical personality traits inherent in most post-WWII families.

Lisa, the eldest, was the classic dark and brooding teen drama queen. She was the first to experiment with drugs, sex and rock 'n' roll. For a time, in the fashion of "girl interrupted," she was held in a hospital in Maryland. To add that she has led a productive and meaningful life, raising three wonderful children, would only be fair. I felt her struggles in our youth deeply, as her closest ally and friend.

Kevan was the classic goody two shoes. She was everything a daughter (or son) should be. She was highly motivated, academically superior; never a stain would she bring to her family. She strove desperately to do all the right things that would gain my father's approval and praise, while at the same time despising him for the very things that made his opinion so important.

I was the physically challenged one. Born with a club-foot, suffering from petit mal epilepsy and dyslexia, and stuttering so badly I could barely speak, I was nothing for my father to be proud of. As the first-born male in the family, my father had high hopes for me. I was an utter disappointment. A poor student, unable to keep still, an inferior athlete, I was thin and not competitive. I had double vision, due to a lazy eye, so I wore glasses. I needed constant tutoring and was at best a D student.

It didn't help that English was the fourth language I was exposed to, and that by the time I was nine, I had already been raised in many conflicting cultures, namely Japanese, French, and Latin American. I became the dreamer, lost in my own world, turning inward to find what I couldn't on the outside. I embraced my mother's Native American heritage, learning

Indian spiritualism, and developed a gift for music, writing my first song at age ten. When she died I was just beginning to establish the close relationship I had always craved with my mother, but which seemed forever out of reach.

David, nine years younger than I, was afforded only the leftover scraps of attention. He was perhaps the most needy, and the youngest to feel the devastation brought by Watergate and the death of our mother. At the tender age of 9, he lost everything that he hadn't yet realized he had. Shipped off to live in Miami with his Godfather, the ex-Bay of Pigs leader Manuel Artime, he quickly found solace and purpose in the glamorous life of rich Miami cocaine dealers. After years of family separation, he soon lost all memory of the mother that had cradled him in her arms and sang to him softly. Whereas I and the other children have memories of our mother crystallized in time that never ages, David has nothing. For each of us, growing up in this family carries different pains and perspectives. I can't know what it meant to be my sisters or my brother, and it is in this realm that truth shows its variables and shades.

December 1970 – Just before our lives changed forever. Taken in Potomac, MD at "Witches Island" l-r Lisa, Kevan, David, and me.

With his father in jail, and his mother dead, younger brother David was sent to live in Miami with his godfather, Manuel Artime.

The fact that my father chose to share details of his knowledge of historical events to no one but me may seem ironic and far-fetched to some. But in 1972, when Watergate exploded,

3

my father had already trusted me in helping him with sensitive and illegal tasks: like destruction of evidence, and hiding large sums of unreported cash from the White House. For me, and a trusting nation, Watergate was the portal that led to doors that had been locked and buried, unknown to a naïve public for decades. The proverbial Pandora's Box was opened and the ghosts of the covert past were unleashed.

Watergate led to all things conspiratorial. By its very nature Watergate was part of a much larger conspiracy, already in place, running smoothly, and functioning as if it were standard procedure. The cast of players, already wallowing in the murky world of black-bag jobs, plausible deniability, money laundering, and assassination plots, were there to be assembled. Fueled by paranoia, driven by greed, sustained by fear, those that were in a position to uphold our nation's values ultimately destroyed the almost blind trust that a nation's people had bestowed upon its government. Watergate was the critical event that showed the emperor had no clothes. From the coup in Guatemala, through the Bay of Pigs invasion, the assassination plots against Cuban president Castro, the militant Cuban exile groups and Mafia lords, through the Kennedy assassination and into Watergate, one thread that ran through all these events was a man, my father, E. Howard Hunt.

E. Howard Hunt working on his book *Undercover*, 1973

Certainly he was one of a cast of hundreds, perhaps thousands, going about their jobs on a need-to-know basis. Sometimes, the left hand doesn't need to know what the right hand is doing. In a business where information is power, nobody has all the keys, all the answers, and the truth that they know is, again, a matter of perspective. Presidents Bush and Reagan both used deniability in their defense. "I was kept out of the loop." President Nixon was much less successful in that argument. He paved the way for those that followed him into that office not to repeat the same mistakes.

This of course doesn't mean not to commit crimes, but rather to cover your ass more effectively. My father's importance in these events can best be underscored by reading the Nixon Presidential transcripts of June 23, 1972. On that tape, Nixon said "Hunt will uncover a lot of things. You open that scab, there's a hell of a lot of things ... This involves those Cubans, Hunt, and a lot of hanky panky that we have nothing to do with ourselves ... this will open up that whole Bay of Pigs thing.... It's going to make the CIA look bad, it's going to make Hunt look bad, and is likely to blow the whole Bay of Pigs thing."

H.R. Haldeman wrote in his memoir, *The Ends of Power*, that when Nixon referred to "the Bay of Pigs thing," he was actually referring to the Kennedy assassination! It's hard now, in retrospect, to think how I felt about the events that were unfolding with dramatic and merciless ferocity back in 1972, like a freight train out of control, unstoppable, smashing everything in its path. I think I must have been in shock, unable to contemplate or verbalize the meaning of what was happening both to my family and to the country.

That my father had been in the American intelligence services for 27 years was something I had learned in 1970 when I was 16. At the time, the term CIA really didn't have much meaning to me, so when he told me he was retiring I didn't think much of it (later, he admitted to me that he was in fact still working with "the Company"). My parents told me that his new job was as a public relations executive for the Robert

Mullen Co. This as it turns out was another front for the CIA. I had grown up believing that my father worked for the State Department, and this was supported by several documents he had hanging on the wall of his office in the basement of our home.

My mother, I had been told, was a retired worker for the Spanish Embassy in Washington, D.C. I remember the stories she told of being on the last train leaving Shanghai, China, as the city fell to the Communist forces. I had even seen the pearl-handled .25 caliber automatic pistol she carried hidden on her body somewhere: pretty exciting for an embassy employee. She talked of having traveled to India, where she spent some time in Calcutta and Delhi, and she had worked for Averell Harriman tracking Nazi money through Europe. This sounded all too confusing to me, but I am sure my father would have had a clearer picture of what she actually did before they married. Once they tied the knot, she became a normal housewife and mother to her children ... or at least that was the story. I can't really tell the facts from the fiction, and that is the sad part of it all. Growing up in a world of half-truths and lies, where it turns out that just about everything you thought was real isn't, and then hearing about her being in the CIA and how they were the "classic" agency couple, using their superficially normal life as a cover for more sinister deeds ... all that stuff. I wish I knew what my mother really did. I suppose it doesn't make any difference any more; she was loving, sweet, patient, compassionate, very artistic, and yet unhappy, tortured, and chronically in pain (she broke her back twice).

She had first married an alcoholic French count of some kind; he was later killed in an automobile crash (maybe, who knows; certainly not I). Somehow, between growing up on a farm near Dayton, Ohio, and joining the "foreign service," she transformed herself into a world-class jet-setting beauty. She was exotic looking; dark thick hair with a widow's peak, strong high cheekbones, and a well-developed full-busted figure. She was German and Sioux, and her Native American heritage shone in her richly olive toned skin. In the year before she died we became very close, and she was able to confide things about her sorrows that I never dreamed existed.

In the waning months of 1970, my father had many new friends at our rambling 14-acre estate in Potomac, Md. Set back from the road, the only visible sign was one that read "Witches Island." Follow that up a dark, unlit one-lane gravel road, and our one-story brick house would eventually appear. We had a front and rear paddock, horse stables, four beautiful horses, a large "pigeon coop"

Dorothy, beautiful and a spy, tracking hidden Nazi assets in 1940's Europe.

the size of a single-wide trailer, a rabbit hutch, and no home would be complete without a bomb shelter. My father's new friends would come and go for "meetings" and dinners. Some of these men I would later recognize as Watergate conspirators Bernard Barker, G. Gordon Liddy, and Manuel Artime. Later, during the Senate Watergate Hearings, I was called to testify about certain things, and was counseled by my father's attorney to lie about having seen these and other men.

One day, when my mother and I went out for a horseback ride, she told me that Papa was not actually working for a public relations company, but was really working for the Nixon White House, doing some secretive things that had her quite worried. She said that against her advice, he was going ahead with an operation that was being directed at the very highest levels of government. He was now so embedded in this mess that she could not be sure of its operational security. There were men whom she didn't trust. He had gotten in with people that weren't themselves aware of what was required of them, professionally speaking. "Amateurs" she said angrily. "Your father, as smart as he is, can't see the forest for the trees."

I had heard them fighting at night and wondered what it was about. My parents rarely fought. I was curious, and one day when they were gone, I sneaked into their bedroom at the rear of the house and looked around. I found some ID's with my fathers' picture on them, but the name was not E. Howard Hunt. It was Edward J. Hamilton. I also found a reddish wig. This is the famous wig that my father was reported to have worn when he interviewed Dita Beard for John Mitchell, Nixon's infamous attorney general.

In 1971, my father's work took a different turn; one that sent him away from home and mired him deeper into the quicksand of Watergate. I didn't really take much notice of his travels, he had spent so many of my formative years away from home, but recently his trips were short and there was tension with his departures and arrivals. Later, I learned that he had gone to Miami to recruit Watergate's Cuban break-in crew; to Los Angeles, to break into the office of Daniel Ellsberg's psychiatrist; and to Milwaukee, to break into the apartment of Arthur Bremmer, the man who tried to assassinate presidential candidate George Wallace. In retrospect, it's a wonder that my father allowed himself to be used in such blatantly illegal schemes. I find it hard to believe that someone who held the notions of our Republic so dear, and the ideals of democracy in such high regard, would be swayed by such obvious presidential paranoia. This must have been the source of the tension and arguments that he and my mother were having.

Chapter Two

WATERGATE DAYS

In the summer months of 1972, my mother took my sister Kevan and my little brother David for a month-long vacation and sight-seeing tour of Europe and England. Lisa was spending the majority of her time with a boyfriend, and I was dividing my time between my band and my girlfriend. My bedroom at home, which my father had built, was in the basement, and when the lights were turned off it was so dark, you couldn't see your hand in front of your face.

Being alone in the house night after night with my father didn't bring us any closer together, and I missed my mother and brother very much. Our live-in housekeeper, an asthmatic English woman, would prepare meals and leave them for us either in the oven or the refrigerator. We rarely ate together or saw each other much, and the house felt overly large and gloomy. When I did see him, he seemed very distant and pre-occupied. I could often hear my father tapping away at his old Royal typewriter in his office next door to my room. He somehow managed to write and have published dozens of spy thrillers. His books were usually published under pseudonyms, and for one series he used David St. John. The only interest we really shared was music, and I remember fondly that he let me accompany him to Blues Alley, a favorite night-spot in Georgetown.

Politically we were much different; he, in my mind, was a right-winger, and I, in his mind, was a left-winger. The truth, once again, is a matter of perspective. I wasn't really a radical. My hair was longish and I didn't support the war in Vietnam, but I wasn't out there throwing rocks or carrying signs. When our family was invited to attend a White House function at which we would be introduced to President Nixon, I quietly declined, stating that I disapproved of his foreign policies. Needless to say, my father was very, very upset.

Sometime after midnight June 17, 1972, I was catapulted out of a deep sleep when the stygian darkness of my basement room was shattered by a shaft of light. My father, silhouetted in the doorway, was calling to me.

"Saint, Saint John! Wake up!"

He flicked on my light and stepped quickly to the center of the room. I sat upright and looked questioningly at my father, slowly focusing on his face. He was perspiring heavily and seemed extremely agitated. His breathing was quick and shallow as he talked in short bursts, pausing to search for the right words. At that early morning hour in the darkness of my bedroom, I had no way of knowing that this moment would forever change my life. For our family and so many others the world was about to turn upside down, and there would begin a bond of secrecy between my father and me that would last 35 years. He stood in my room, suit jacket rumpled and shirt-tail hanging out. He swiped his hand across his face and loosened his tie.

"Papa, what's the matter?"

"Saint, I need you to get dressed and come upstairs immediately!"

"Yeah, okay ... what's going on?"

"I'll fill you in when you're more awake ... right now I need you to do exactly as I say, and not ask any questions! Do you understand me?" He was firm and direct, and I obeyed him without hesitation. I'd never felt really needed by him before, never felt very important. Now, here was this man for whose approval I had deeply longed; and he was asking for my help! What would any good son do? I didn't have time to think that I was becoming part of a crime, a conspiracy to destroy evidence. It wouldn't have made any difference anyway. Starved for his attention, I happily did what he needed me to do.

He turned and left the room. I hurriedly got dressed and ran upstairs. Walking back to my parents' bedroom I knocked lightly on the door and my father opened it. He had taken his jacket and shirt off and was wiping himself with a damp towel. Wordlessly he motioned me in, and I saw that there were two suitcases on the bed.

"I'm going to ask you to do something for me tonight and you must never, ever tell anyone about what happens here. Can I count on you?"

"Yes, of course," I responded.

"First, I want you to get some rags from the garage, grab some of those dish-washing gloves, and some ammonia or window cleaner. Then come back here." I followed his instructions and gathered the requested items. When I came back to his bedroom he was talking on the phone, but I couldn't hear what he was saying. He placed the receiver back in its cradle and told me to open the suitcases up and remove all the items. What I saw was a jumble of cords, wires and electronic stuff, some walkie-talkies, cameras and a small collapsible tripod. It had obviously been thrown together in a hurry. I removed the items and placed them on the bed next to the suitcases. "Put these gloves on and start wiping everything down with the glass cleaner. When you're finished, put it all back in the cases and wipe them down too. I'll be back in a minute to help you."

He put on a clean shirt and left me alone in the room. I think he headed down to his office in the basement to make some more phone calls. When he returned he had a small stack of envelopes and papers in his hand. He tossed them down on the bed next to me, and I noticed some of them were written on White House stationery. He sat down on the other bed, put some dish gloves on and started spraying and wiping the remainder of the equipment. I may have been young, but I did realize that I was erasing fingerprints. That much I knew.

When we were done he said, "Now we have to get rid of this stuff, we don't have much time ... it looks like it's getting light out." Noticing that I wasn't wearing shoes, he said, "Get your shoes on and meet me in the garage in five minutes!" I ran down to my basement room, put my shoes on and left, turning out the light and closing my door. I trotted through the house and out the kitchen door where my father was already placing the cases into the trunk of his Pontiac Firebird.

Slamming the lid down, he motioned for me to get in. As we pulled out of our "Witches Island" he turned left onto River Road. It was still dark as we drove silently, my father lost somewhere in his thoughts. I can only imagine what was going through his mind. Was he making a mental check-list of everything he needed to take care of? Was he wondering about his safety? Would he be found out? What were his men doing? How long would they keep silent? He was going to have to get money to secure their bail. They were going to need legal counsel. A million things must have been racing through his mind and as I drove with him, I too was lost in thoughts of my own. I was scared, exhilarated and still completely in the dark about what was going on.

We drove for about 45 minutes to an hour and then turned west towards the canal. This was a small waterway that served this part of Maryland a hundred years ago. Barges and small vessels plied their trade goods on its waterway, providing commerce and transportation long before there were any decent roads. Now, as dawn cleared the night from the sky, we found a good spot near the edge of the water. My father turned off the engine and waited for the silence to signal that all was clear. He got out of the car and removed the suitcases from the trunk. Walking to the edge, the water flowing lazily along, he tossed first one, then the other out into the muddy canal.

Full daylight was shining around us with the temperature and humidity rising as we drove back down River Road to our house. On the way back, my father said that he had been doing some special work for the White House. Last night he had been on an assignment when things had gone sour, necessitating his quick departure from the scene and his abrupt return home. "I don't know what's going to happen, but I may need your help with some other things."

"Okay, Papa," I said.

"Let's turn in and get some shut eye. I think we're in for a long day." I headed downstairs, threw myself on the bed and fell asleep.

My mother, sister and David found out about Watergate in the papers over in England. They called and planned to return as soon as possible. I'm not sure about the timeline here because I know it was at least several days before they returned. In the interim, I was to help my father out with a few more tasks. One involved the transfer of a large amount of cash from a safety deposit box in a Georgetown bank to a secret hiding place in the basement of our house. The plan was this: I was to wait several hours after my father left and meet him at a pre-arranged time in the safety deposit room of the Riggs National Bank in Georgetown. Watergate had been in the papers, and from what I later learned, the FBI was looking for my father. I don't know if this is true or not, but supposedly he was the object of a huge search. Agents were scouring the planet. How they could have missed him hunkered down at Witches Island, I'll never understand. I guess his home was too obvious a place.

I drove through the windy hills of Potomac and into Georgetown, an affluent shopping and historical site near Washington DC. Pulling into the parking lot in my little Chevy Monza, I checked my watch: 2 pm. Right on time. Wearing a suit jacket as instructed, I made my way to the vault area. Ringing the bell, I was allowed into the safety deposit room. My father was to meet me at 2:10, and in a few minutes he arrived.

"Did you notice if you were being followed?"

"No, I didn't" I replied. He removed a box from the wall, opened it, and pulled out a large manila envelope. Turning me around, he lifted up my jacket and stuffed it down the small of my back.

Then he said, "Good, you look fine. Take your time driving back, make sure you're not being followed, and when you get home go down to the basement. Unscrew the heating duct above your door, and shove this in."

Again, I blindly did as my father wished. I left the bank and headed back to the house. I kept an eye on the rear-view mirror, and as instructed, took my time in reaching my destination. Several times when a car seemed to shadow me from behind, I turned around and doubled back. I thought I may have picked up a tail, so as I approached Potomac Village, I turned into the shopping center and parked. Watching the suspected vehicle make a turn down Falls Rd., I was confident that I had outwitted them. It was getting hot, and the envelope under my shirt was soaking up my sweat. By 4:30 I was back at Witches Island. I busied myself unscrewing the heating duct that my father had told me about. He had left a three-step ladder nearby for me to use. I shoved the envelope into the space as far as I could, and replaced the sheet metal covering. My father came home a few hours later and thanked me.

We had dinner together that evening, and I asked him how much money was in the envelope. "Not nearly enough," he said quietly, "about a hundred and fifty thousand dollars. I know that sounds like a lot of money, but it has to be dispersed to a lot people." I asked him about the newspaper articles that I had seen about the break-in at Democratic National Headquarters. I recognized some of the names as men who had been to our house that summer. Trying not to upset me, and perhaps believing in the power and loyalty of the men he had been working for, my father told me he was confident this was all going to be resolved soon, and everything would get back to normal. It wasn't clear to me what "getting back to normal" meant, but I was glad to accept his views.

There was one more bit of dirty business that my father would have me do for him. Late that same night, he came down to my room carrying an old Royal typewriter, like the one he used to write his novels. He set it down on the floor and banged it several times with a hammer. Producing a cloth sack, he placed the mangled typewriter inside. Handing it to me he asked me to take the sack and dump it into Griffith Pond, a small fishing pond located in the middle of a huge field directly across the road from our property. It was owned by a General Griffith and boasted a huge southern-style house at the top of a very long driveway. I had never met the General, but he allowed us to ride our horses in his fields. I remember with great fondness how my mother and I rode through the tall grass around the pond and through his woods. He must have had at least a hundred acres and our mother brought each of us children there to ride. I also spent many afternoons there, fishing with my brother David.

Unlike our property, the General's was easily seen from the road, so, on that warm, clear night I slung the sack over my back and hopped the fence. Keeping a low profile, so as not to be caught in any car headlights that might be flashing by, I made my way to the edge of the pond. Without a second thought I hurled the sack into the middle of the pond where it obligingly disappeared into the depths. Many years later in Miami, my father and I revisited the tale of the typewriter, and it was then that I learned why he got rid of it. The machine had been used to forge bogus government cables linking the assassination of Vietnamese President Ngo Dinh Diem to the Kennedy administration.

Within a few days, my mother returned and now she became the one to help him through the maelstrom. As it turned out, this sealed her fate and led directly to her death. My mother, always thinking of us children, took three thousand dollars from the envelope and gave it to me. I gladly took the money and headed out across the country in my van, taking my girlfriend with me, and thinking that everything would blow over by the time I got back. I was in for a serious disappointment when, after a month and a half, I returned.

United Flight 553 Crash in 1972

United Airlines Flight 553 crashed on its approach to Chicago Midway International Airport at 2:28 p.m. CST, on December 8, 1972. After the crew was told to abort their first landing attempt, the aircraft struck trees and then roofs before crashing into a house. A total of 45 people were killed in the accident.

The three-man flight crew died along with 40 of the 55 passengers. The crash destroyed five houses and damaged three others, killing two people on the ground.

Along with Dorothy Hunt, also killed were Illinois Congressman George W. Collins and Michele Clark, a correspondent for CBS News.

Chapter Three

TRAGIC ACCIDENT OR MURDER?

I returned to madness; I knew from reading the papers in California that Watergate hadn't gone away, but I was wholly unprepared for what awaited. The scandal had developed into a cottage industry. There were reporters from seemingly everywhere camped out at the foot of our driveway. It was a media circus to rival any of more recent times. We drove into the driveway and everyone jumped up, shouting questions. We drove out of the driveway and everyone jumped up, etc. In and out, up and down! We were virtual prisoners on parade.

As Watergate deepened, my mother served as the unofficial spokesperson for the jailed burglars. Nixon's personal lawyer, Herb Kalmbach, hired ex-New York City Police Dept. Intelligence Unit officer, Tony Ulasewicz to funnel "hush money" to the many men that so depended on him. Using codes like "the writer" (my father), "the writer's wife" (my mother), "the players" (the burglars), and "the script" (the money), more than four-hundred-thousand dollars were paid out. How much of this went through my mother, I don't know, but she did have many spooky rendezvous at dimly lit bus terminals and airports, where locker keys were taped in secret locations.

She was worried that she would be kidnapped or worse. I know this because she told me so. She felt like she was being tailed, and probably was. I can only reflect that she was an incredibly brave woman. Charles Colson called my mother a very "savvy" woman. She was frightened, under tremendous pressure, and deeply involved in some very serious business with some of the most dangerous people in the world. My father was viewed as a blackmailer, and my mother the instrument of his bidding. She was out there, by herself, making demands, playing it tough, meeting desperate people in lonely, dark places. She listened, I imagine, to every sound around her ... footsteps echoing down empty streets. She watched shadows moving across vacant buildings. She noticed strangers glancing a little too long, or too quickly. She made her way through basement car garages, always checking her rearview mirror.

The need for money was almost suffocating. Calls from lawyers, banks, brokers, and debts piled one on top of another ... and another and another. School bills needed to be paid, the car payment was late, and the children's school tuition was overdue. Multiply this by all the families whose fathers had been jailed for the Watergate burglary, add to that the need for repayment and good faith gestures, and you can begin to see what kind of pressure she was under. I saw in her face such utter depression, such loss of hope, such fear and anger. Oh, the resentment, and the bitterness! She suffered from severe pain due to having broken her back twice. She worried about her weight gain, and suffered from diabetes. She had spoken to me several times of divorcing my father, and just when she decided to make the break, this disaster happened.

This Watergate monster was like an iron chain around her neck with the weight of the world attached, and it robbed her of her freedom. She had to stay now. She couldn't leave her husband at a time like this. So, she endured. She not only endured, she fought tooth and nail. She rose to the challenge and faced all the pressures and demons of the nation's angst. Yet, throughout all of it, she tried her best to keep a smile for her children. She never lashed out, never grew impatient, never withdrew. On the contrary, she reached out even more. I don't know if she knew the end was near, but she worked at being our friend. Each of us will always have the memory of stolen moments, of shared secrets, and deep conversations. This was a new woman to us; she opened up about herself and her dreams and losses. She had suffered through ten pregnancies; six ended in miscarriage, and four babies lived.

Summer 1972, Dorothy Hunt in England
while Watergate made headlines in the States

By December 1972, time seemed to have run out. My parents had made a desperate play to gain back control of their lives and those of the loyal Cubans. The "writer and his wife" had made a final demand to the President of the United States: pay up, or we're going to blow this whole thing right up in your face. They had the evidence to link the President to the Watergate scandal, and perhaps to deeper and darker things. Nixon, caught on his own secret tapes, wanted to pay off Hunt at all costs. He figured it might cost "… a million in cash. We could get our hands on that kind of money," he said. On December 8, 1972, my mother boarded United Airlines flight 553 scheduled to take off from Dulles Airport, non-stop to O'Hare airport in Chicago. The purpose of her trip has generated a lot of controversy. The facts are:

> 1] She was to meet with her cousin's husband, a man named Harold Carlstead, who owned two Holiday Inns in the Chicago area.
> 2] She was delivering a large sum of money.
> 3] Some of the bills could be directly traced to the Committee to Re-Elect the President.

19

4] She also carried with her almost two million dollars in American Express money orders, travelers checks, and postal money orders, according to testimony before the National Transportation Safety Board during the re-opened Watergate plane crash hearings, June 13-14, 1973.

5] United Flight 553 never made it to O'Hare airport. My mother and 44 others were killed.

As the big jet closed in on its destination, the pilot received a call to divert the plane and land on the little-used and much more poorly equipped Midway airport. As it approached the outer runway marker lights, they flicked off, and, mysteriously, the pilot was not able to communicate with the tower. Missing the landing strip, the plane tore into the surrounding houses, demolishing several, and came to rest amid huge fires, with pieces of wing and metal housing strewn in  a debris field which some have described as a scene of total destruction and absolute hell. Miraculously, the outer markers returned to perfect working order moments after the crash. The radio control tower also seemed to have suddenly started working again. What's even more remarkable is that within minutes there were 50 FBI agents at the crash site. The fire department was called within a minute and a half of the crash and yet when they arrived, they were told to stand down until the FBI was finished in their search. What were they searching for? The nearest FBI field office was twelve miles away. How could there be 50 agents at the crash site in such a short amount of time. On June 13, 1973, Chairman John Reed of the NTSB told the House Government Activities Sub-Committee that he personally sent a letter to the FBI. It included the following:

a) Never in its history had the FBI acted as it did in the flight 553 crash investigation.

b) Under what authority did it act? (Air piracy was later cited.)

c) Before the NTSB investigators could do so, the FBI conducted 26 interviews within 20 hours of the crash and an FBI agent had gone into the tower immediately after the crash and confiscated the tape recording relating to the flight.

On December 9, 1972, just one day after the crash, White House Aide Egil Krogh was appointed by Nixon as Undersecretary of Transportation, supervising the NTSB and FAA, the two agencies investigating the crash. Also on Dec. 9, White House Deputy Assistant to Nixon, Alex Butterfield, was appointed the new head of the FAA. Five weeks after the crash, another of Nixon's men, Dwight Chapin, became a top executive at United Airlines. Am I to believe that all these facts are just random coincidences? All of this, as well as testimony from eyewitnesses on the ground that said the plane seemed to explode before it hit treetop level, pretty much defies the laws of chance. I was taught that if something looks too good to be true, it usually isn't, and if you smell smoke, there's probably a fire.

This suspicious plane crash is still one of the greatest mysteries surrounding the Watergate scandal. I call upon the U.S. Congress and the Department of Justice to reopen the case, and, using our modern technology, re-investigate it for possible sabotage and a subsequent cover-up.

The photo in Rolling Stone Magazine
of Lisa and I, at the foot of our
driveway, in Potomac, Md. Dec. 1974

Chapter 4

THE END OF WITCHES ISLAND

The loss brought about by my mothers' death was almost unbearable. My father was being held in various jails, and at best we only spoke with him briefly over the phone. When we could, we visited him in jail. Without any experience in living on our own, Lisa, David and I did the best we could. One day, lawyers came to Witches Island and told us we would have to move out in 60 days. The house needed to be sold to pay attorney fees and we should start packing and looking for somewhere to live. If things weren't bad enough already, my father had some kind of stroke after being attacked in a D.C. Jail.

We worried that he wouldn't make it, and for a time he was put on suicide watch. Lisa and I packed up the house as best as we could; it was so hard to do, with so many memories of our mother and the life we had as a family that lay among the empty boxes and cartons that littered the loveless house. Lisa, fragile and waif-like, cried endlessly, and nothing I could say or do would console her. We tried to cheer each other up by talking about how we'd find a lovely small house. Lisa was adamant about living near a certain bridge in Kensington. She was vulnerable and unprotected, with nerves strung tightly by lack of sleep and too much worry.

We did our best to take care of little David, only nine years old, so young and so lost. I think he must have suffered more than any of us. With so much sadness around us, we became inseparable. Then one afternoon Lisa came home after house hunting, shouting with joy; "I found it, I found it, our perfect little home!" We danced and held each other shouting, "We found a home, we found a home!"

That joy was fleeting: attorneys came and took David away. The only explanation they gave was that they (my father) felt it would be a better environment for him if he moved in with his godparents in Miami. This would prove to be a huge mistake: Miami would soon be the cocaine capital of the world, and David was right smack in the middle of it. He would be raised with few good influences and no real love. Now living alone and feeling betrayed by everyone, Lisa and I stayed on in the house. We kept the lights low at night, and sat up late talking and crying, holding on to nothing but each other and the darkness that enveloped Witches Island.

In 1973 we appeared together in support of our jailed father at the Senate Watergate Hear-ings. Our pictures, splashed across the front pages of news-papers worldwide, showed us embracing the very man who had inadvertently destroyed everything in our lives. We fi-nally did find our little house and tried to put things back together, but nothing would, nothing could, be the same. The warm afterglow that was the memory of our mother stayed with us, and we felt her spirit everywhere.

Lisa and I would faithful-ly visit her grave: first, every weekend, later, every month, and slowly, we left her alone.

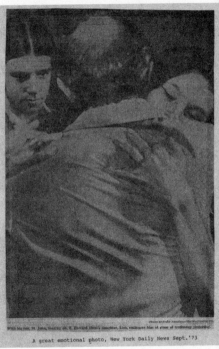

With his son, St. John, looking on, E. Howard Hunt's daughter, Lisa, embraces him at close of testimony yesterday

A great emotional photo, New York Daily News Sept. '73

She rests is a small cemetery near Potomac, Maryland. The pastures and woods that she so loved to ride through have all been bulldozed and turned into shopping malls and parking lots. No one has been to see her in decades. It's sad to me. The truth is that it's just a stone with a name carved on it. She lives in my heart and soul and in my dreams. I see her sometimes, and I know I will see her again.

Chapter Five

PICTURE ON A POSTER

My father served 33 months in federal prison, the longest stretch at Danbury, Connecticut. Frank Sturgis, the Cuban freedom fighter, arch nemesis of Castro, plotter in assassination attempts, and co-conspirator in Watergate served his sentence at Danbury as well. It was after my father's incarceration that the first accusations surfaced allegedly linking him and Sturgis to the murder of President Kennedy. I remember quite well how I first heard of this.

I had moved to Oakland, California and got a job driving a delivery truck for a local bakery. I stopped by a pay phone on my route, and as I was dialing the number something caught my eye. A familiar face stared at me from a crudely printed poster on a phone pole. It was my father! His was among several on a poster that read "CIA KILLED JFK." I dropped the phone and carefully removed the poster. Back in my delivery van, I looked at what it said. Below the large heading, it showed six photos of at least three men; my father,

'CIA Killed President Kennedy' — Jim Garrison,
New Orleans District Attorney, who investigated the assassination, see Oliver Stone's 1991 film 'JFK'

Immediately after the assassination of JFK, Dallas police arrested three "tramps" in a railroad gondola behind a grassy knoll and picket fence, where numerous witnesses swore they heard gunshots, saw commotion and people running. Two of the "tramps," photographed by newsmen, looked like Watergate burglars, buddies and CIA operatives, E. Howard Hunt (below, left) and Frank Sturgis (right). The FBI, according to Ronald Reagan and Nelson Rockefeller, released the "tramps" without taking any arrest record, fingerprints or mug shots!

In 1975, the Rockefeller Commission issued a report which, without publishing the photos, declared, "Even to non-experts it appeared that there was, at best, only a superficial resemblance between the [pictures of the] Dallas 'derelicts' and Hunt and Sturgis." *Time* (11/24/75) echoed this lie. In 1979, at the Hearings before the House Select Committee on Assassinations, which also whitewashed the coup d'etat, Dr. Clyde Snow, a forensic anthropologist testified, "There is some indication that Hunt underwent plastic surgery [to bring his] rather protruding ears closer to his head."

If Hunt & Sturgis killed JFK, then why doesn't President George Bush, former Director of the CIA, appear on TV and admit there was a coup d'etat in Dallas, November 22, 1963? Because, as Pres. Johnson told Earl Warren, Chief Justice of the U.S. Supreme Court: "If, after a probe of the facts, some [innocuous] conclusion wasn't reached as to who was responsible for the assassination ... [there would be] social breakdown."

HUNT   TRAMP A   HUNT   STURGIS   TRAMP B

Rats investigating the mice covered up the coup d'etat: President Ford (Freemason, Council on Foreign Relations); John J. McCloy (Rockefeller's lawyer, chairman CFR & Chase Manhattan Bank, involved in WWI & Cuban missile crisis) and Allen Dulles (CIA, Pres. CFR) served on the [Earl] Warren (V.P. running-mate of Dewey [R], 1948) Commission in 1964 and; C. Douglas Dillon (Kennedy's head of the Secret Service & Treasury); President Ronald Reagan, Gen. Lyman Lemnitzer (33° Mason, advocate of nuclear war in Vietnam; planned "Operation Northwoods" to kill Americans and blame it on Cuba to get U.S. into war to overthrow Castro see, *Body of Secrets*, James Bamford, 2001); Lane Kirkland (AFL-CIO, funded strikes that toppled Chile, British Guiana, Poland), Erwin Griswold (Nixon's Solicitor General) and John T. Connor (Director Chase Manhattan, Pres. Johnson's Secy. of Commerce, CFR) served on the [Nelson] Rockefeller (largest stockholder of Chase Manhattan, bankroller CFR, Ford's VP) Commission in 1975. Where was George Bush Sr.? (See *The Nation*, July 16 & Aug. 13, 1988 or *Lane* op.cit. below.) The plutocrats had many motives to murder JFK. **The CIA caused coup d'etats throughout the world — so why not Dallas!**

No one with seizeable assets says Hunt was one of the "tramps" because Hunt sued two publishers for that alleged defamation (see attorney Mark Lane's 1991 book, *Plausible Denial*) and we need someone to refute Dr. Snow's HSCA testimony, which ultimately exonerated Hunt. Sen. Edward Kennedy can't demagogically rally the people or other Senators for a "palace coup" because he has no solutions ... there would be disillusion, revolution ... social breakdown.

Sources: *Coup d'Etat in America: The CIA and the Assassination of JFK*, M. Canfield & A.J. Weberman, 1975; *On the Trail of the Assassins*, Jim Garrison, 1988. © 1992 **By Bruce A. Friedemann**

Frank Sturgis, and a third I didn't recognize. Below my father's picture was someone who looked like my father, only older and dirty. Below Sturgis' picture was one of someone who looked a lot like Frank except older, and the third man had the same photo twice, but one from a different angle. The copy below the photos proclaimed, "E. Howard Hunt; convicted Watergate burglar and CIA assassin in 1974 and in Dealey Plaza in 1963." The poster advertised a lecture the following day in San Francisco by Dick Gregory and was sponsored by a group calling themselves the JFK Investigating Committee or something like that. I was in shock! I could barely make it through the rest of my route. I didn't know what to think. I felt sick to my stomach. I couldn't believe something this bad could be happening to my family again! Hadn't we paid enough? Hadn't my mother died for the sins of my father? Why would these people think such a thing? Where would it all end?

After I settled down, I began to think back and try to remember what happened the day Kennedy was shot. Surely this would clear up the question and perhaps I could attend the lecture and clear my father's name, but as I thought about it, I began to feel a sickly, creeping suspicion in the pit of my stomach. I remember very well that I was nine years old and in the fifth grade at Brookmont Elementary School when they announced the news over the loudspeaker. Soon afterward, school was dismissed. I can't remember how I got home, whether I was picked up, or took the bus, but when I arrived my mother was there and she was very upset. I tried to picture my father in the house that day, but couldn't.

Then, like a bullet exploding in my brain, I remembered my mother telling me that my father had been in Dallas! I can't place the exact time she told me or if she was speaking in reference to the assassination, but I clearly recall her telling me this around that time. It may have been before, but I also remembered something strangely coincidental; my father elected to have some sort of plastic surgery done to reduce the size and change the shape of his ears. In my mind these events occurred roughly at the same time. I looked at the poster, studying it over and over again. I thought of going to the lecture but chickened out. I didn't want to know any more details or speculations. In the photos of the tramps, the one that is supposed to be my father looks amazingly like him. He has a very distinct nose and the shape of his mouth is also quite distinctive. I felt strongly that this could be him. Now, years later, we all know that the true identity of these tramps has been discovered due to the diligent research of devoted Kennedy assassination researchers. But for years, the accusations went on and on. Still, some feel that my father never told all of what he knew regarding this tragic chapter in our history.

My father always maintained that he was not involved in the assassination and didn't know anyone who was involved. He maintained that he firmly believed Lee Harvey Oswald acted alone and without any involvement from any intelligence agency, with the exception of the KGB. This is laughable; anyone who's read the CIA's own reports knows that Oswald had connections to the CIA and the FBI. The fact that he, a U.S. Marine, defected to Russia at the height of the Cold War and then returned, with no apparent consequences, is reason enough to draw suspicion. I wrote my father a letter asking him about the poster and its accusations. He wrote back to me that, "As you well know, I was at home that day, and we watched the news broadcasting the unfortunate events until late in the evening when you children went to bed. I was in the house all day."

Later, under oath, he would change this story several times. He testified that he had actually been at work that day. He left the CIA office and drove home early. Later he changed it again,

saying that he had stopped by his favorite Chinese grocery store to purchase some items for a home cooked meal. Still, he maintained that he was with his children throughout most of the day. When asked what the name of his favorite Chinese store was, he couldn't remember. He did offer that it was located on a certain street in Chinatown in Washington D.C. When investigators checked all the Chinese stores in the city, none were close to that location. My father testified that he had been seen at work that day by one of his co-workers, yet when that co-worker was cross-examined, he could not specifically recall seeing my father, he only thought he "might" have seen him.

How could a man whose life was in the intelligence business not be able to recall, without fail, where he was and what he did on the day that the President of the United States was murdered? How is that possible? Why did he change his story so many times? If his children were his alibi, why wouldn't his defense team call us to testify for him? This could have put the whole matter to rest once and for all. Why? Because it was a lie; I was at our home that day, and I never saw my father. That's not saying that he murdered the president, but it does serve to underline the maze of lies and plausible deniability that was our life. I never spoke to my father about these outrageous contradictions, and he never addressed this topic ... at least not until later ... years later.

Chapter Six

THE OUTLAW LIFE

While the rest of the world was consumed with Watergate, I was consuming drugs. First, when my father went to prison, I stole his bottles of Quaaludes and obliterated the anguish of the loss of my mother with heavy doses of the hypnotic. I have a photograph that someone took at the house I shared in Kensington, Md. with my sister Lisa. In the photo I can be seen passed out under the coffee table in our living room. Friends I am still in touch with remember how they often picked me up off the floor and laid me out on the couch. This could only have lasted a month or two because soon my father's stash ran out. And, as I recall, he had quite a few bottles.

When I was a child, my father freely offered drugs as an answer to various needs I may have had. When I was tired, he'd offer me half of a Dexedrine tablet. If I was restless, he'd hand me some Librium or Valium. So it was a natural progression to turn to drugs. My parents weren't boozers, aside from all the cocktail parties, otherwise I might have had a drinking problem as well. But that's one demon I've never had to wrestle with. Alas, there is still time.

I started taking LSD when I moved to Wisconsin. I read the Tao te Ching by Lao Tzu, and dropped acid with my girlfriend and band mates. We were young, and the whole world was an experiment. We found a source for the highest quality "window pane" acid and brokered a deal in Milwaukee. We traded an eighteen-wheel flatbed truck's worth of aged barn boards for a candy jar full of the finest, purest and strongest four-way Owsley Acid in the country. We took the drug religiously and while the summer nights were warm and the sound of mosquitos whined in the air, we sat on top of a high hill overlooking our farm house and watched the scenery dissolve into liquid beauty. An average trip lasted 12 to 18 hours. I "traveled" thousands of inner miles, and I don't think I came down for two years. I have many amazing stories about LSD ghosts and entities. Timothy Leary would have been proud of me!

From Wisconsin's natural beauty, I moved with my band and girlfriend to Oakland, California. The great acid was all gone and cocaine was the rage. Like everybody else, I started experimenting with street-grade cocaine. I found it an unproductive drug. Still, it was fashionable. It wasn't until my brother David moved out to live with me in nearby Concord that I first tried high-grade Peruvian flake.

What a difference! David had been busy at his prep school running cocaine and call girls to his schoolmates. He had limos parked outside of his dorm on a 24 hr. standby service. He wasn't even eighteen yet! There are some incredible tales of drug excess and endless days of sex from those crazy times. David and I were a toxic and dangerous combination. We pushed each other into deeper and darker corners of abuse, neither one wanting to surface and deal with the issues that propelled us into that downward spiral. I'm sure we came as close to death as anyone can.

Throughout this time, David had a series of girlfriends, and I was hooked up with some young sisters. I had met them on the streets of Berkeley and invited them out to our house. After the three of us started having sex, we hardly ever left each other's company. We went everywhere and did everything together. The girls' appetite for fun and games would have crippled most men, and when cocaine-fueled sex marathons left me too wasted, I would invite my brother to take over as sex master of these two nymphs. The stories we could tell would surely deserve a triple-X rating.

One classic scene will have to suffice. One evening I took the girls to an exclusive Italian restaurant in Concord, a very expensive and highbrow place. We snorted coke on the table during dinner, and a number of hundred-dollar tips helped induce the waiters and other service people to stand around trying to shield the dessert from the other patrons: fellatio from one of the girls, who had crawled under the table. Many other nights, David and I could be found at another local establishment, drinking Long Island iced teas and snorting coke.

Eventually, of course, the glamour of "toot" wore off, and the paranoia set in. David had moved into his own place and was doing big deals in the coke world. He had his Miami connection: Cubans and Columbians. As the world watched *Scarface*, David lived it. He was a big spender. He had lawyers and entertainment stars as clients. He flew coast-to-coast setting up deals and raking in the money. He carried a gun and had weapons stashed all over the place. One time as he got into my 1965 Mustang, his 9mm. went off and shot a hole clean through the drive shaft. We both kept an arsenal which included police-style sawed off shotguns with clips, semi-automatic weapons, nunchakus, shuriken throwing stars, and a variety of knives and lethal weapons.

The next drug of choice for me was methamphetamine. This was like discovering dynamite after playing with firecrackers. I soon followed in David's footsteps and built a lucrative meth business in the Bay Area. I didn't like the image of high roller, instead favoring a much lower profile. Over the years, I dealt an average of several pounds of 90% pure product a month. At one time I was moving at least a pound a week. I had two partners who were hard-core bikers: Dirty Dan and Big Don. They rode BMW's and were not associated with the Hell's Angels.

We did, however, buy from and sell to the Angels numerous times over the years. They never bothered us, and we respected who they were. We dealt straight and never burned anyone. We had our own lab, which eventually produced as much as 300 lbs. But, after years of successful outlaw living, I was eventually and inevitably busted.

I lived through an attempt on my life as the result of an inside betrayal. Briefly, I was set up to be robbed. The gangsters came to my home and beat me until I was almost unconscious. They dragged me into my house, tied me up, and prepared to torture me with boiling water if I didn't reveal the location of my drug stash. Before they could get the info out of me, Big Don came to my door and let himself in. Seeing me tied and beaten, he whipped out his .45. The thieves ran out of the house as Donny fired at them. Later, after we determined who they were, Dirty Dan and Big Don sent one of them to the hospital severely beaten. The other was arrested for unrelated robbery and drug charges and went to San Quentin.

I was never comfortable with the enforcement end of the drug business, so I left that part of it to my partners. I heard stories from them that would curl your toes! I was a meth addict until 2001, when I changed my whole life. I quit drugs, stopped dealing and took my family away from the Bay Area with all its reminders of that outlaw life.

Chapter 7

SUMMER 2002 – 2003

In the summer of 2002 I learned that, after being hospitalized for many months, my father was still very sick, weak and in need of a leg amputation. His prognosis was poor and he was resisting the idea of being without one of his legs. He was suffering from vascular degeneration in his left leg, and although he'd had several operations already, nothing could save his gangrenous limb. My brother David had been staying at the family house in Miami and trading shifts with Laura, my father's second wife, at the hospital. She had practically been living there and was near exhaustion. My father had met Laura while in prison, they married in 1977, and had two boys, Austin and Hollis.

David was due to fly to Las Vegas for a new job, and I decided it was time to see my father before his condition worsened. If he refused the amputation he would surely die. Embittered by the past, emotionally estranged to his eldest daughters, and not wishing to be a burden to Laura, he was tired and unable to cope with the challenge that amputation would present. I understood this, and wouldn't have blamed him if he chose death. He had, after all, lived a long and fruitful life, albeit notorious at times.

I found a two-for-one flight on Southwest and decided to bring my four-year-old son Travis to meet his infamous grandfather. This might be the only opportunity to do so, and I hoped seeing the youngest member of our family might cheer him up enough to reconsider his situation. Upon arriving in Miami, David picked us up and we had a brief reunion of our own. The next day Laura drove us to the hospital and said that although very weak, Papa was excited about seeing me and meeting his grandson. At the hospital, Laura waited in the hallway with Travis, and I walked into the dimly lit room. I was shocked by his appearance. He was emaciated and his breathing was slow and labored. The skin on his face sagged as if he were already dead. I walked quietly over to his bedside and sat down. I was overwhelmed by his terrible condition as I fought to gain control of my emotions. "Papa," I placed my hand in his, squeezing it gently. "Papa, its Saint John." He opened his eyes slowly and I felt him grip my hand.

"Saint, it's so good to see you. Laura told me you were coming." His voice was weak but his grip was stronger than I expected.

"Papa, I'm so sorry this is happening to you."

"You know about my leg? They want to take it off."

"I know ... Laura told me." He pulled back the sheet and revealed his damaged leg. There was a huge scar, from his ankle to his groin, and his leg was swollen and purple. "Oh Jesus," I said.

I held his hand and spoke very quietly into his ear; my face pressed against his. "Papa, you are the patriarch of this family. You are deeply loved and needed by all your children. Losing you would be catastrophic for all of us and we just need you and love you so much. I know this is hard but you've had hard times before. You're the rock of Gibraltar and I don't think that Mama would want you to leave us yet. There's so many things that we haven't said or talked about." I could feel the wetness of his tears against my cheek and I too began to cry. As our tears intermingled, he gripped my hand in an embrace that sought to end all the anguish that had been the focus of our life. "I love you so much Papa," I said softly into his ear.

"I love you too, son." As his grip weakened, I sat up and said "Papa, there's someone I want you to meet." "Travis," I called out. "Travis, come here and meet your grandpapa." Laura slowly opened the door and Travis came into the room and I lifted him up onto the bed. "Papa, this is your grandson, Travis."

Though weak and emotionally drained, he lifted his head a little and said, "You are a handsome boy." Travis looked at me and asked if Papa was going to die and I said no, he was going to get better. I slid Travis off the bed and Laura took him out to the hallway. After they left, I sat quietly next to my father and reflected for a moment on all that had happened. He had lived a remarkable life, and if this was his choice in dying, then it was up to all of us to carry on. I thought he was sleeping but he called my name softly. "I'm here, Papa." I said.

"I've had some things on my mind ... I ... need to ... tell ... talk to you when I'm not so tired.... Maybe we can talk tomorrow. Will you be here?"

"I'll be here Papa," I said.

"You know I've always tried to do what was ... what I thought was for the best ... I didn't know what would happen ... your mother knew ..." His voiced trailed off, and I kissed him on the forehead. The following day I came back, but he slept mostly and we never got the chance to speak in private. I left a day or two later and when I called Laura to check on his condition, she told me that he had decided to allow the amputation. This was a brave man I thought. I don't know if I would have made the same choice if it had been me. I respected him for it. Time passed and the operation was a success. He had two amputations: first at the knee, then farther up. His health started coming back and he seemed on his way to recovery. This was short lived, and I was to hear many times that he was back in the hospital with complications: pneumonia, or high fever. It seemed like death was stalking my father, but he just wasn't ready to give up. When I visited my father in August of 2003, he was doing better. Although he was restricted to his bed and his wheel chair, his spirits lifted when I arrived. He was still quite fragile and tired easily. He refused to work with his prosthetic leg, saying that it was just too much effort for someone his age.

I spent time watching television with him and on really nice days, I pushed him around the neighborhood in his wheel chair. Laura worked as a teacher and both his other children had busy schedules, allowing lots of time for Papa and me to talk. It was on one of these days when the air was thick and humid that we found ourselves talking about Watergate and the help I provided him when he needed it. I was glad he recognized what I had done for him, yet I really wanted to talk about the cost to our family. This was a painful subject and one that had rarely, if ever, been discussed. My father had a selective memory when dealing with the trauma of the past, and as I prepared to transfer him from his wheelchair to his bed, I pressed the conversation. I started to explain that I had spoken several times to my sisters in an effort to reconcile some of the bitterness they felt towards him. It was no secret that Kevan and Lisa both blamed him for our mother's death, the disintegration of our family and the emotional damage that had left them with so much anger and hostility. I had tried to explain that forgiveness was the only way to heal these wounds, but they seemed unwilling to make the first move. He sighed heavily and said he appreciated my efforts but with so little time left, he doubted that anything would change. What did he mean by, "So little time left?"

"I have prostate cancer, Saint."

"How long have you known?" I asked.

"About a week, but they're still running some tests; we're hoping it can be treated with radiation and drugs." I couldn't believe what I was hearing.

"Does anyone besides Laura and me know?"

"We haven't told anyone yet, and I want you to promise you won't say anything until we do."

"I promise." Then he said this:

"When your mother was killed, I feared for your lives ... I wasn't sure of anything, and I didn't know what would happen to you children. Things were out of control and I couldn't protect you. Your mother was everything to this family and as long as she was alive, I knew things would be all right. When she died, I knew that I had to keep quiet about a lot of things ... things that I don't feel good about ... some things are better left alone."

The words struck me like a semi-truck. Never in all these years had my father referred to her death as anything but an unfortunate accident. My father had a near genius's command of the art of spoken language, and he picked his words very carefully. To hear him suggest that my mother was murdered was a sign that something monstrous, something evil had happened. The hair on my arms and neck stood on end and I felt the specter of death floating past me. I pressed him for more.

"If you need to talk about anything Papa, I'll just listen ... maybe it would be good to get some things off your mind."

"You know I've been unable to write anymore, and I had hoped that our lives would be better, financially speaking, than they are. I've never really gotten much for my novels and I'm just too old to write another book now." I knew that he was living beyond his means and that Laura's salary and his pension from the CIA was not enough to provide for his family the way he'd hoped. "There are some things I could write about and it's not like people haven't tried to get me to talk about Watergate and Kennedy."

"What do you mean?" I asked.

"Well for example when Oliver Stone asked me to join him on the set of the Nixon movie, I agreed to do so, as a consultant. I flew out to California with Snyder [my father's lawyer] and your brother. I met Anthony Hopkins and some of the other actors and writers on the set. Stone took us all out to a lavish dinner, and I found him very irritating as he persisted in grilling me over JFK's murder. Finally I looked at him and said, 'I'll be willing to tell you everything you want to know about JFK's murder if you'll pay me five million dollars!'"

"Are you serious? Would you really do that for five million dollars?"

"Well, I would, but no one took me seriously. I did however hear from one of Stone's writers several times offering to write a book about my life. I think his name is Hamburg, Eric Hamburg ... a nice guy really and quite modest. He's kept in touch every so often but I'm not sure how much money he can offer." I listened to my father letting him move the conversation wherever he wanted to. "Did you know that Kevin Costner flew down to the house here to see me?"

Chapter Eight

SECRETS REVEALED

David Giammarco is a Canadian television personality and author of a coffee table book on the James Bond movies. My father became acquainted with him when Giammarco interviewed him on the failings of the CIA in the aftermath of 9/11. When Giammarco was working on his Bond book he asked my father to write a short introduction. Unfortunately, my father was too ill to write, so Giammarco wrote the intro himself and gave my father credit. This was a nice gesture, which my father deeply appreciated. In the course of their friendship Giammarco mentioned that Kevin Costner was one of his best friends. Costner, as we know, starred in the Oliver Stone film *JFK*, and had since become somewhat of a conspiracy enthusiast. Giammarco prodded my father about the assassination and Papa told him the same thing he'd told Oliver Stone: If the money was right, he would tell all he knew.

Later, in an incident that I was unaware of for over a year, Costner and Giammarco had flown to Miami to discuss what my father thought was a film project about his life. When they arrived at the house Laura and Austin were there, and after some small talk Costner blurted out "So, tell me Howard, did you kill the President?" They sat stunned for a moment, and my father finally said, "I don't know what you're talking about." The meeting ended and Costner left without getting the story.

There were several things wrong with his approach. First of all he should have never asked my father anything about JFK in front of Laura and Austin. Laura would have never married my father if he'd admitted to having any involvement or knowledge of the Kennedy assassination, and I think she would have divorced him if she found out he'd been lying all those years. Without Laura to care for my father, his life probably wouldn't have lasted as long as it did. Secondly, Costner should have been prepared to discuss a ballpark dollar amount and, thirdly, he didn't take the time to get to know my father or for my father to get to know him. Costner came across as just another opportunist looking to make a buck. He was insensitive to the fact that the events in my father's life, including the JFK period, had destroyed his first family and he was very protective of his second family. So, I have to wonder: was $5 million the magic number that would ease family pain?

Before I returned to California I got Giammarco's address and phone number from my father's Rolodex and decided to write him a letter. My reasoning was purely selfish; I had been working on a memoir and thought that Giammarco would be useful in helping me find a publisher. I wrote to him, and he called back saying that, from a marketing point of view, if my father were willing to go public with the information he felt sure about concerning JFK's murder, it would give my book a greater chance at success.

At this point my father had only hinted to me that he had secrets. This didn't surprise me; his whole life had revolved around secrets. To keep a secret all you have to do is keep quiet; to protect a secret you have to lie. I knew a few facts; that my father had been accused and questioned about the JFK murder; he had denied under oath any knowledge; he had lost a court case in which he was unable to satisfactorily establish that he hadn't been in Dallas on Nov. 22, 1963. A witness had testified that she had seen him in Dallas handing out envelopes of cash to Frank Sturgis, and, whether my father admitted it or not, he was a key figure in just about every sinister covert operation from Guatemala, the Bay of Pigs, the assassination attempts on Castro, to Watergate. I also knew that my father had made a career using disinformation, plausible deniability, and dirty tricks. He had well-known links to the Cuban underground and shared their deep hatred for Kennedy. How could he not have inside information on the assassination of JFK?

Something else clicked; the cryptic words my mother had said to me: "Papa was in Dallas." I swear upon her memory that she told me this. Could there be another explanation? Maybe, but I don't know what it is.

I told Giammarco I would give it some thought. As a word of encouragement I told him that if my father were going to trust someone it would be me. I composed a letter in which I implored him to reveal to me what he knew, if anything, about JFK's murder. Aside from the monetary gain, I tried to appeal to him on a deeper, more personal, level. After devoting his life to the service of his government, he had been abandoned by those he trusted and served under. He had been imprisoned and stripped of his dignity. His name had been dragged through the mud by the media in connection with all manner of terrible things. His principles and his patriotism had been challenged. He lost his wife, and his family had been damaged beyond repair. Authors had profited by using his name to sell their conspiracy stories. He had never been appreciated for his own writing talents. Even though he was published some eighty times, the stain of Watergate and the media portrayal of him as a bungling burglar and second-rate writer had forever marked his career. Now, in his last years of life, shouldn't he marshal his strength and get back at everyone by finally telling the truth? Didn't he owe it to himself, the Nation, and his family to leave a legacy of truth instead of doubt?

I sent the letter off and waited for a reply. A few days passed and then Laura called me. "Saint, your father wants to talk to you." I could hear Laura hand him the phone and then he said

"Saint, in regards to your letter ... this is something that I'm not averse to, however you need to understand that my time and cooperation is directly proportional to the financial prospects."

"I understand that, Papa. Papa ... are you there?" The phone went dead and I hung up. Conversations with my father were often one-sided; he was so deaf toward the end he couldn't hear me on the phone and when I talked to him in person, I had to shout. He would often nod in agreement even if he couldn't really hear you. I called Giammarco and spoke with both him and Costner about my father's willingness to talk to me. My plan was to fly down to Miami and evaluate what information my father knew and report back to them. I wasn't sure at this point what he knew. Flying was not something I was fond of and even less so when I realized that my flight was on Dec. 7, 2003, one day short of 31 years since my mother's plane crashed. Laura picked me up at the airport.

"Your father's been in the hospital for a few days ... high fever and loss of appetite, but he's home now and I know he'll be very glad to see you, Saint." I dropped her off at her school, drove to the house and let myself in. Austin and Hollis were both out of the country, so I knew I'd have some one-on-one time with my father. I didn't discuss the reason for my visit with Laura because I knew she would be against dredging up all the bad old stuff. I wondered how my father would be able to cooperate with this project while keeping it a secret from Laura, but I decided to leave that up to him.

Pushing open the bedroom door, I walked quietly over to my sleeping father. He looked frail and gaunt, but as I placed my hand on his, he woke up. "Papa, its Saint."

"Saint, so good to see you. Is Laura here?"

"I dropped her off at school. We're here alone."

"Good, let's go into the kitchen. I'd like to have some soup. Are you hungry?"

"I'll have some soup with you." I transferred him into his wheel chair and pushed him into the TV room, where he liked to watch Fox News with the volume up full blast. I prepared some soup and we sat watching TV and discussing current events. "Papa, can we talk about my letter?"

"Okay, why don't you take me back to my bed in case Laura comes home early? We don't want her getting upset by this."

"How are you going to work this out; I mean with Laura?"

"Well for the moment, she's willing to let us talk as long as she doesn't hear anything unpleasant. She believes what I told her: that I don't know anything about JFK's murder."

"I think Laura's very naïve about the darker side of politics." I added.

"Well, that's one of the reasons I love her so much." he said. "Now let's understand that what I tell you must be kept in secrecy and you'll never reveal any of this without my approval. Understood?" I nodded in agreement and wheeled him back to his bedroom. I made him comfortable, and this is what he told me.

Frank Sturgis

David Morales

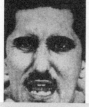

Antonio Veciana

William Harvey

Cord Meyer

David Atlee Phillips

In 1963 my father and Frank Sturgis met with David Morales, a contract killer for the CIA, at a safe house in Miami. Morales explained that he had been picked by Bill Harvey, a rogue and unstable CIA agent with a long history of black ops, for a secret "off the board" assignment. It was Morales' understanding that this project was coming down through a chain of command starting with vice-President Lyndon Johnson. Intrigued, my father listened on.

Harvey had told Morales that he'd been brought in by Cord Myer, a CIA agent with international connections, who in turn

43

was working with David Phillips and Antonio Veciana. Phillips was CIA station chief in Mexico City and deeply involved in the dangerous world of the Cuban underground. Veciana was the Cuban founder of the violent Alpha 66 group, bent on overthrowing Castro by any means necessary. All these men shared common ground: a hatred for Kennedy. He was dangerous to their vision of America's political future, and had abandoned them in their time of need by refusing to bail out the Bay of Pigs fiasco.

Cord Myer had his own reason to hate John Kennedy. His ex-wife Mary was one of Kennedy's numerous mistresses, and the gossip surrounding them infuriated Cord. After the assassination, Mary Myer was mysteriously murdered and her personal diary stolen from her apartment, allegedly by James Angleton, chief spook of counterintelligence. The rumor was that Mary Myer had kept detailed notes about Kennedy and perhaps had information about his death.

Of the men mentioned thus far, my father knew Cord Myer, David Phillips, Frank Sturgis and Bill Harvey. He'd never met nor heard of Morales until that night and claimed he'd never heard of Antonio Veciana. This seems unlikely. Alpha 66 was the leading anti-Castro faction in the Cuban underground. David Atlee Phillips worked with my father closely and was actually recruited into the CIA by him when Phillips was working as a journalist in Santiago, Chile. When Lee Harvey Oswald allegedly visited the Russian Consulate in Mexico City in the summer of '63, Phillips was station chief there. Although Phillips denied ever meeting Oswald, Antonio Veciana gave evidence that he had met with Oswald and his case officer, a man known to him only as Maurice Bishop, in Mexico City. Although unwilling to identify Phillips as Bishop, Veciana did provide a detailed description of Bishop to a sketch artist and the resulting drawing looked very much like Phillips. I sat by my father's bedside and asked, "What happened then?"

"Well, I asked them what this assignment was."

Sturgis looked at Morales and then at my father and calmly said, "Killing that son of a bitch Kennedy." My father said he was stunned, but I don't think he would have been that surprised; getting rid of Kennedy was a common topic of conversation among the Cuban exiles. The truth of the matter is that Kennedy was also hated by much of the military-industrial complex. He was viewed as soft on Communism, and many factions of the government, the exiles, the Mafia, and millions of racists were looking to get Kennedy out. My father then simply asked, "You guys seem to have enough people, what is it you need me for?"

"Well," Frank said, "you're somebody we all look up to ... we know how you feel about the man. Are you with us?" My father looked around the room for a minute and said, "Look, if Bill Harvey has anything to do with this, you can count me out. The man is an alcoholic and a psycho."

"You're right," laughed Frank, "but that SOB has the balls to do it." The meeting ended, and my father thought it nothing more than the usual "Death to Kennedy" ranting.

The next day when my father and I were alone in the house, we discussed ways that we could divulge certain information to Giammarco and Costner without giving anything away. My father came up with a good solution: put it in code. With that plan in mind, my father provided me with a hand-written diagram outlining the chain of command, a list of people who were involved, and a descriptive time line of the events that led to the "Big Event." This was the code for JFK's murder. The Greek alphabet provided the code for most names, such as "Nu" for LBJ, "Beta" for Cord Myer and so forth. He also wrote a few pages of background material on Sturgis, Phillips, and Cord Myer. The reason for this was that he wanted me to type out a descriptive outline in code form and fax it to Giammarco. Hopefully it would be enough to initiate a formal agreement and a good faith payment. My father wanted $150,000 to be deposited in an account. In view of the fact that Costner and Giammarco had been dangling a multi-million dollar figure for a documentary, a book, and DVD sales and rentals, I didn't think that $150,000 was too much. I had to wait until Laura was out of the house to type it up and fax it off.

Before I returned to California I had one more conversation about JFK with my father. He related to me that it was his understanding that Oswald had in fact fired on the President that day, but there was also another man, a French assassin,  firing from the famous grassy knoll. The man's name sounded something like Sarte or Satre, and he may have been recruited for the job by Cord Myer, who had connections to the Corsican underworld. In his own diagram, my father outlined "French con. Man ... grassy knoll."

Lucien Sarti

Chapter Nine

WINDOW OF TRUTH

The window of truth opened and closed so quickly that it barely created a breeze. If I hadn't been there, no one would know. If I hadn't heard my father's voice with my own ears, his words would have dissipated like the early morning mist on an autumn blacktop road. Even scarier, the information regarding the "Big Event" would never have been spoken in the first place. I had conspired – we had conspired – to tell the truth. I had approached my father in a once-in-a-lifetime moment, when he felt that death was at his door and it was time to tell the truth. In a few brief days he laid out the "chain of command," as he put it, laying the blame on the doorstep of LBJ.

I didn't realize that my presence was essential to the fruition of his confession. After I left for California, the "Miami Mafia," as I call his second family, slowly chipped away at his resolve. Like a man drowning, he reached for me and I wasn't there. How could I have known? It's true, we had these secrets, and I thought that we would follow through. This was to be his final mission. It was supposed to be our mission. In conversations we had, he said that he realized this was going to be a significant story. He was confident that, based upon the information he had thus far provided, we could interest an agent and eventually get a sizable advance. He made it clear to me that there was more to add to the story as long as financial remuneration was forthcoming. He swore me to secrecy, and revealed that he was somehow going to have to work this out with Laura.

I knew this was going to be a problem for us, yet I was naïve enough to think that he would be able to work it out. Laura is a very sweet and politically naïve person. She comes from a very strong Southern moral background. In conversations I've had with her she reacted with disbelief that the CIA condones political assassination. She's told me many times that she married my father with the strict understanding that he had no knowledge of such immoral and evil acts. My father also told me that he had sworn his innocence of CIA/JFK plots to her. The problem my father now faced was how to break the news to Laura without losing her. How could he tell her after all these years that he had been lying? How would his family react? Laura had made it very clear to me that all the money in the world would not be enough to compensate for the disgrace this would bring. She was very adamant in her threat to leave my father.

In retrospect, I wonder if she would really have left such a needy old man if he had followed through with the truth. Papa had been denying any knowledge of these matters for years. After all, he had testified twice in court that he knew nothing of the assassination. I wonder, though, was Laura suspicious? She certainly became suspicious of my intentions. When my father went to court in the Mark Lane/Liberty Lobby trail, Laura was at his side. She watched helplessly as he was subjected to merciless examination by Mark Lane. She must have wondered why witnesses were testifying that Howard Hunt was in Dallas during the assassination. I think Laura must have had suspicions about the JFK thing but, like a good wife, she stood by my father, and he stood by his story.

All of this weighed very heavily on my father. Once I left, the pressure was on. Not only was this worrying him, but he told me that he had caused so much pain and humiliation for his first family, that he was deeply troubled by what the fallout would bring to his second family, raised long after Watergate and the JFK assassination charges had disappeared from the headlines. Every once in a while there would be the odd Watergate anniversary interview, but Austin and Hollis basically hadn't been affected by these events. He had made sure to shield them from the adverse publicity that had destroyed his first family.

He gave up his lecture tours and settled on a life of relative obscurity and safety. He wrote frequently and continued getting published at the rate of almost two books a year. I never understood how fame eluded him. Not only fame, but respect from the journalistic world. Perhaps it was the stain of Watergate. He had been publicly discredited when his memoirs came out in 1974. After initial publication, his testimony at the Watergate trials showed that he had lied in at least ten instances in the book. It was pulled from the shelves and quickly disappeared from circulation. It is interesting to note that he barely discusses the JFK assassination there. He all but leaves it out.

Laura never knew about my father's turmoil over this until I told her in the year before he died. As a matter of fact I never knew it until my father's attorney Bill Snyder revealed it to me. *Secrets* ... Papa had a habit of keeping them. Full disclosure was a completely foreign idea.

Following my trip to Miami, I set up a meeting with Bill Snyder at a restaurant in Sausalito, California. During our lunch, Snyder was "amused" that Howard had any information at all regarding the JFK assassination. He recounted that this had been something that Howard had been approached with before. Snyder told me that, as Howard's counsel, he would have to recommend that Howard not speak of such things. He would be jeopardizing his freedom and it was a strong possibility that he could be prosecuted. "Even if prosecution were not to happen," Snyder said, "he would face considerable harassment and humiliation from the media and public." Snyder insisted it was a grave mistake to go down the assassination conspiracy trail. "Look what happened to Oliver Stone," he said. When the meeting was over, I knew Snyder was going to be a problem.

As I drove back to Eureka, California, where I was then living, I realized for the first time that this project would have to overcome some serious opposition. There would be pressure on my father from Laura, Austin and Hollis as well as Snyder and possibly even Kevan to abandon this project. I was right. I just didn't know how bad it would get.

Father & son, Miami 2002.

Chapter Ten

THE LAST CONFESSION

In January of 2004, I got a letter from my father expressing concerns that the project was moving too slowly: "The last I heard of our would-be sponsors they were preparing papers ... it is high time a good faith transfer be made. Without that, I don't want to talk or negotiate something intangible. I have two stipulations: source of info must not be identified; and any and all legal fees arising from the enterprise must be paid by the sponsors. Having said that, I look forward to seeing you here. Much Love, Papa." Later that month I received a Fed Ex package containing a cassette tape. The following is a condensed version of what was on the tape. His voice was extremely labored, and he gasped many times as he fumbled with the tape recorder or the microphone.

"LBJ had designated Cord Myer to undertake a larger organization while keeping it totally secret. LBJ settled on Myer as an opportunist like himself, a man who had very little left to him in life ... ever since JFK had taken Cord's wife as his mistress." He spoke about Sturgis and Morales and the Big Event. At the end of it he said, "Let me point out that if I had wanted to fictionalize what went on in Miami and elsewhere during the run-up to the Big Event I would have done so, but I don't want any unreality to tinge the information ... that I've provided to you and you alone ... what's important is that we've backtracked a chain of command up through Cord Myer and laying the doings at the doorstep of LBJ...I'll be perfectly willing to expand on some of these matters in the future ... I'll only do so if there is adequate monetary motivation. Please understand that."

Once the contract from Costner came, with no mention of "adequate monetary motivation," I knew the deal was off. At best they offered an equal partnership to be divided between Costner, Giammarco, and my father, but an equal partnership for what? Costner wanted me to fly back to Miami and bring my father out to Los Angeles to film a documentary, with Costner acting as the interviewer and my father answering his questions. I spoke with Costner one last time and told him this was an insulting offer and that my father would never reveal to the world what he knew without being paid well. I never asked for any money for myself. I wanted this for my father, and of course the prospect of writing and publishing my own story sometime in the future. Laura called and Papa asked for all the paperwork and notes as well as the cassette.

So what's the truth? As I wrote at the beginning, the same truth can be viewed from many different angles. The way I see it, my father built his life around secrecy. He was in many ways a key to a mystery, a thread that links and binds the CIA, Bay of Pigs, assassination plots, JFK, Nixon, and Watergate. I had hoped that he, as one of the last men standing, would have the last word; but he kept most of his secrets. This is not your average family story … it's the story of a man and his son; a family torn apart by scandal and lies, betrayal and murder, patriotism and treason. There is a woman who gave her life trying to secure his redemption. There is an old man dying a slow death, a family without love, and a son who will never be forgiven for telling this story.

Chapter Eleven

THE WINDOW CLOSES

After the failed Costner project, I believed that none of this information would ever be revealed. I was disappointed and frustrated at how this had turned out. I know my father was disappointed, yet he was willing to drop the whole thing. His health was continuing to decline, and the thought of dredging all this up, taping interviews, and dealing with the press was more than he seemed able to deal with physically and mentally. I know he must have tortured himself over the conflicts this would have caused, and it appeared to be with some relief when he asked me to return all the memos and audio-tapes I had. He asked me to promise that I would never reveal these startling details or use this information in any way. Reluctantly, I agreed. Before I sent back the original memos, I copied them. I never returned the audio tape, hoping he would overlook it. He never mentioned it, so I assume he had forgotten that I had this critical piece of evidence. In the next few months, I put all of this behind me and resumed my normal life of school, work and family obligations.

It was during a call from my brother when I told him about the Costner project and what a disaster it had turned out to be. He laughed and told me about how he had spoken with Costner and Giammarco the year before, and Papa hadn't said anything.

Learning more than I already knew, I chuckled when he told me that, apparently, Giammarco and David were party buddies, and Costner and Giammarco were good friends. They had offered a large sum of money through David to Papa if David would set up an interview for Costner. Costner then hired a private jet and flew down to Miami for that ill-fated interview with my father.

My dad thought Costner was coming to discuss a film proposal about his life. So when Costner showed up and bluntly asked him who killed JFK, my dad was surprised, became very angry and declared the visit over. Costner left feeling he had been deceived and soon everyone blamed each other for the whole mess. David was then further sidelined from family and suffered deeper alienation.

As David and I spoke on the phone, I told him for the first time that Papa had revealed details about a plot to assassinate JFK, and that I had copied hand written memos and kept a cassette recording that Papa had asked me to return. David said he knew someone named Eric Hamburg who might be willing to discuss how best to use the information that I had. Eric Hamburg, he said, had been a technical advisor on *JFK*. David had met him on the set of *Nixon*, which Hamburg had co-produced. Papa and David had been invited to watch some of the filming, and they had met Anthony Hopkins, Oliver Stone and Hamburg. Papa's attorney, Bill Snyder, had joined them on the set and later for dinner.

I don't know why my father ever thought that Snyder was a capable attorney. He was not a trial lawyer, and it was obvious even to Laura that he was in way over his head at the Mark Lane trial. As Laura recounted to me later, Snyder was a bumbling, perspiring novice when compared to Mark Lane. She believed it was his lack of experience that had caused my father to lose the case. Still, somehow, my father felt that Snyder was competent because he had asked him to negotiate terms during the Costner project. On the phone, Giammarco, and Costner, made it very clear to me that Snyder was the single most damaging influence during negotiations. At least we were all in agreement that Bill Snyder was no asset to my father. David said he would get in touch with Eric Hamburg and get back to me.

A few days later David called and gave me Hamburg's phone number. I waited a few weeks before I called him, but when I did, he seemed very nice and was interested in hearing this new information regarding the assassination. I quickly realized that Hamburg was no ordinary Hollywood type. His mind operated like a computer on the subject of the assassination. He was a well-respected conspiracy researcher and had been instrumental in pushing through a bill that resulted in the declassification of thousands of government documents. He had been to Cuba several times and met Fidel Castro during a symposium about the Bay of Pigs. Hamburg told me that he always felt that E. Howard Hunt knew much more about the assassination than he had ever admitted.

"A man like your father," Hamburg said, "who was involved in both overt and covert CIA/Cuban plots, was certainly in a position to have known about plots against JFK. It's well known that your father's trail leads from CIA through Cuba, the Bay of Pigs, plots to kill Castro, and Watergate. I've always felt that your dad was the thread that linked all these events, and possibly the hit on JFK."

"My father never admitted to me that he had any part in the JFK murder" I said.

"Well what is it that you know?"

We had a long conversation in which I revealed to him what my dad had told me. He confirmed that some of the conspirators were well known in JFK conspiracy circles and some were not. Of these, Hamburg said Cord Myer had never been offered as an actual conspirator. The LBJ connection was fascinating, he said, and noted that this was a major piece of the puzzle. "Do you think you could get your Dad to tell you more?" "Jesus" I said. "I just don't think he's willing to get into this all over again." I told him about the Costner project and we ended our conversation with the understanding that I would try to find a way to approach my father.

Miami 2003 – The day Father told me the truth about JFK

Chapter Twelve

GLIMMER OF HOPE

In February 2005, I wrote to my father with the idea that if I could pitch a new project, one with less emphasis on the JFK material, we could interest a writer who would be willing to co-write my father's true story as a lasting legacy. In this letter, I outlined that we would want to explore all the details of his fascinating life: "[They are] interested in writing about your whole life; childhood, education, family history, war service, OSS, CIA, prison, etc. ... they are also interested in the fact that you turned to me in your time of need during Watergate, how we carried out several ops of our own, what happened to us after our family was destroyed.... This is far more to my liking than the Costner project. The part of the story in which you were offered a role in the Big Event, but wisely turned it down, is just a footnote in your amazing life and although it is still a commercially strong selling point, would not be the focus of the project. Please consider coming to this project and working with me and whichever writer can offer us the best deal. It would be a cherished memory for a son to have."

During March I got a phone call from Papa approving the basic principal of the project: to co-write a truthful memoir with details regarding Watergate and JFK that had never been made public. After a month of negotiations with Eric Hamburg, it was agreed by the three of us that Hamburg and I would fly down and tape a lengthy interview with Papa to be used as material for the book. Luckily, my father's health was fairly good at the time, and he seemed enthusiastic about the tapings.

In April, Eric and I met at his hotel in Miami to discuss questions for the interview. Eric was very well prepared and had outlined each principal area to be covered. He had pages and pages of names and questions that pertained to all areas of interest: OSS, CIA, Bay of Pigs, Guatemala, the White House, the Plumbers, Watergate, and of course the JFK assassination.

I spent nights at my father's house and we met with Eric in his hotel room at the Holiday Inn on Miami Beach. Laura was happy to see that Papa was enthused about something. "Saint, you do your father a world of good by coming down here," she said.

"Well, I'm so happy to have something for him to work on."

Austin was somewhat less enthused. I think he had his suspicions about our ideas for the book. We scheduled 2-3 hour tapings at the Holiday Inn, which included a break for lunch. Papa was amazingly clear-headed and answered all the questions with great interest. Each day when I returned to the house with him, Laura and Austin bombarded me with questions. They wanted to know what was going on behind those closed doors. We weren't talking about JFK stuff were we?

I said we hadn't gotten that far yet, but we would be going over that ground in the next day or so. After Papa went to bed, Laura, Austin and I had a meeting. Austin wanted to make it clear that asking questions about the JFK assassination was not what they wanted me to do. I said, "I think that part of Papa's life is very relevant and is something that I think he needs to talk about."

"Saint, you don't seem to understand that nobody here wants you to discuss these matters, whatever they may be, with Papa." Laura sat quietly looking on while the tension level rose quickly.

"Austin," I said, "you don't seem to realize that these events ... Watergate, JFK, and my mother's death ... all happened to a part of this family that you have nothing to do with! These events had a direct effect on my life, and there are secrets that I share with Papa that he wants to reveal; and quite frankly I just wish all of you would stop pressuring my father into doing what you want him to do. You should be giving him the courage to do what he wants, not holding him back for your own selfish reasons!"

"St. John, we trusted you when you said this was a different project. We now feel that you still have intentions of having your father discuss matters that could become huge problems for him and our part of the family. We think you're the one who is selfish and narrow-minded. You're not thinking of what might happen to us and to your father if he starts talking about all this secret stuff." I felt like I was being attacked and I was getting really angry.

"Look, I said, do you think Papa is guilty of killing JFK?"

They sat stunned! "You're joking right?"

"No, just answer the question!"

"You're asking me if I thought my, uhm … our father killed JFK?"

"That's exactly what I'm asking you."

"No, we don't. There's no way Papa would ever have done something against his own President … his own country."

"Well, I don't either!"

"You don't?"

"No, I don't. I do believe he knew about some plans to get rid of Kennedy, and he's told me so. I think it's valuable information both historically and for the book." Laura, who had watched quietly as Austin and I battled each other, shifted in her chair and said, "St. John, I think you really do believe that your father had something to do with JKF's death; just like you think that your mother's death was a murder and not an accident."

"Laura, those are two different, but possibly not unrelated, events. There are things that Papa has told me which cause me to believe that he has had his suspicions as well." Then I said, "You guys are all living this fairly perfect little life down here, and I come down threatening to upset your perfect little world by wanting to find out the truth about my father! I'm sorry it upsets you. It has been deeply upsetting to me for over thirty years. My life was almost destroyed by the things he did, and although I'm only blaming myself for the way I lived my life in the years that followed, I just want to know the truth about who my father and mother were!" I was fighting back tears now, but I continued. "So unless you find some way to stop me, Papa and I are going to continue to tape his life story, and whatever he decides to say is what it will be." I stormed out of the room and out the door. The Miami warmth, the moon and palm trees helped me to calm down.

The next morning as I got Papa ready for the trip to Eric's hotel room, I didn't talk about our fight the night before. I especially didn't want Papa to see evidence that this book project was already dividing a family that desperately needed to heal. On the way to the hotel I asked Papa how much of what he had told me last year in the memos he would be willing to talk about on camera. He turned in his seat and looked at me perplexed. "How much does Eric know?"

"He knows the bare bones stuff. He wants to ask you specific questions about Sturgis, Cord Myer, Morales and those guys."

"Jesus Saint, I thought you promised not to tell anyone?"

I breathed deeply and sighed. "I think it's a very strong selling point to your book. Can't you just tell Eric what you told me?"

"I'm getting a lot of pressure from everybody to not go into that stuff."

"Who's doing it?"

"Well, Laura is going to be very upset and it could ruin our relationship. You know she forgave me for my infidelities several years ago, but I had to really win her back. I was younger then and I've been so sick ... lost my leg ... and she's the only one that really takes care of me. She's all I have and I probably wouldn't be alive this long if it weren't for her. Austin is embarking on a Naval career and may eventually decide to branch out into intel. I think these revelations might have an undesired effect on his chances."

"Do you feel that, or is it just Austin saying that?"

"Well, both of us really."

"Who else?"

"Snyder is bringing up all these potential legal problems we might encounter ... I just don't have the strength to engage in those types of confrontations and court appearances anymore."

"So what's the bottom line Papa? Are you going to talk about it truthfully or not?"

"Well, if I'm not asked, then I'm not volunteering anything."

"And what if you're asked?"

"I can't promise you honesty. I'm deeply sorry, but that's the way it's going to have to be. I can't and won't jeopardize this second family that I live with for something that has already created problems that are only going to get worse. Saint ... I lost my first family and wife over some of this stuff ... if I bring it all out now, I may ruin more lives. Don't you understand that?" He reached over and held my hand firmly. I was moved to tears to see how conflicted he was about this. "I love you son, and I respect what you've tried to do here, but I just can't give you what you want." I sat quietly next to him and allowed the silence to shield the pain. It was obvious that he was making a choice – a choice I had presented him with. It was them or me and so far they were winning.

As we pulled up to the hotel in silence, I felt very badly for Eric. He had come all this way and although there had been no promise that my father would deliver the goods, I knew Eric was going to be disappointed. When I knocked on Eric's door I asked him if he could excuse himself and allow my father and I to have a few minutes alone. Eric seemed a little bewildered but gave us our privacy. I wheeled my father over by the window and asked him one more time about the Big Event and Mama's death. He just closed his eyes and shook his head in the negative. I felt very bad for Papa. I felt bad for myself, as well.

Miami 2005 – Relaxing between the exhaustive interviews.

Chapter Thirteen

THE FINAL INTERVIEWS:
APRIL 2005

Over those few days, my father gave Eric Hamburg and I what was to be his final interview. Papa was always an early riser and I would usually find him watching Fox News and drinking coffee when I greeted him in the morning. We drove most often in silence to the Holiday Inn on Miami Beach where Eric had set up an informal taping area. I was keenly aware that these were going to be long and probably difficult sessions.

We started out that first morning with Papa talking about his mother and father, his early childhood and the start of his service during WWII. He was sharp, animated and had an encyclopedic memory of all things. For a man in his mid eighties, he was incredible. The mood was relaxed, and we let Papa reminisce about whatever came to his mind. The interview concluded after three hours when he grew tired and said he wanted to go home. Later that afternoon, when Laura, Austin and Hollis came home, there was much discussion and curiosity about the day's events. Papa was in a great mood and enjoying all the attention he was getting. Austin and Hollis then invited themselves to come over and watch the next interview. This was bad news! With them present, E. Howard Hunt was never going to discuss anything he had confided to me about the JFK assassination.

I called Eric that night and told him the Miami Mafia was going to show up, probably sent there by Laura or Bill Snyder to keep a handle on what Papa was talking about. Eric said we would just have to play their little cat and mouse games; they surely wouldn't be there the whole time.

The next day we picked up where we had left off, and a nice flow began to develop. Papa was getting into some interesting stuff about the formation of the OSS and the early history of the CIA. Suddenly there was a knock on the door and in popped Hollis, just to see her dear old Dad! I was like a cat bristling at an intruder: a female canine intruder! She sat there, smiling pleasantly and holding his hand, the devoted daughter concerned for her Papa. I was nauseated. I wanted to grab her by the throat and toss her out with the laundry. Luckily, this portion of the interview wasn't classified. I hoped this would be her only visit. Papa got tired after a few hours and we broke for lunch. After some delicious stone crabs and a few beers, he was ready to go again. I must say that his enthusiasm and energy were incredible.

After taking him home, I met Eric at the hotel and we planned our strategy for the next round of questions. We realized that the critical issues would be coming up at the next session. We had already covered OSS, CIA, the coup in Guatemala, the Bay of Pigs, and many of the principals involved in those events. I wondered how we could ease my father into discussing the JFK hit. Would he even go there? Would the Miami Mafia show up and abort this most sensitive area? Eric had a huge list of questions. He had seen the handwritten memos that my father had given me and he'd heard the confession tape.

I drove home that night watching the sun set over beautiful Miami Beach and wondered how the next day would unfold. This was perhaps the most important part of the interview. Once back at Papa's home, I tip-toed around looking for some alcohol to drink. I was pretty wound up and really stressed out. I sat there blindly staring at the TV, drinking rum and cokes. I didn't like what was happening. I didn't like the fact that his second family was putting so much pressure on him. They viewed me as an outsider, and I felt the same way about them. This was a battle, a war really; a fight between truth and lies. I wished I could just whisk my Papa away from there. I tried to shut my eyes, but sleep eluded me. Maybe just one more rum and coke would wash away the stress. I drank heavily that night.

The next morning I took Papa to a doctor's appointment and then we met Eric for lunch. The interview got under way and Eric asked him about certain Mafia plots against Castro. Eric questioned him like a good attorney trying to get to the heart of the matter without losing the cooperation of his star witness. When we were just about to get to specifics regarding the JFK stuff, Austin showed up. What perfect timing! I was ready to blow a fuse. Eric was much calmer than I was. My contempt for Austin was thinly veiled. Eric swiftly changed the topic to other, less critical matters. We finished out the session and Austin took Papa home. I tried to imagine what they were talking about.

When I got home later in the day, it was clear that the mood was very bad. The air was thick with tension and nobody was even making small talk with me. I felt like I should sleep outside under a bush. I stayed in my room and out of the line of fire. A few hours later I emerged, hoping to watch a little TV. Papa was back in his hospital bed and wasn't feeling well. He was drained from the day's events, and I wondered if he was going to be able to continue the interview tomorrow. I realized that he was the one being torn apart. I knew it must be excruciatingly difficult for him.

I was feeling a lot of things: anger, sadness, resentment, and frustration. This whole project had already taken so long, and had gone through so many changes that I just wanted it to be over. I tried to talk to Laura and Austin that night, but we blew up at each other. The fear and paranoia had taken over. After a very intense argument about the JFK taboo, I'd had enough of arguing and acting out, so I got up and left. I was an unwelcome person, but it was my father's home, and as long as he wanted me there, I was going to stay. Papa could have terminated the interviews at any time, so I knew at least a part of him wanted to do it. I spent most of that night worrying as I tossed and turned. I must have fallen asleep just before dawn because I could feel the air conditioning kick on as the morning sun sweltered outside. Sleep, I was so happy to sleep!

I woke up with a sense of doom hanging over my head. It could have been the hangover I was nursing, but after a few strong cups of coffee it didn't go away. Papa's mood hadn't changed; he was upbeat and ready to go to the hotel for the final day of interviews. I called Eric and told him we were on our way. I prayed that we would be able to work without interruption. Once we settled into our seats, Eric began questioning Papa about some of the details of the conspiracy to kill JFK. As I suspected, this was not easy. My father denied what he had previously told me. Changing his strategy, Eric asked about Cord Meyer, Bill Harvey, David Morales, Frank Sturgis and Dave Phillips. This was masterful. He was giving my father the means to talk about the assassination without implicating himself.

My father, of course, was equally as cunning in his choice of words. Without the fear of reprisals that would surely have come as the result of a more direct admission, my father freely talked about the JFK murder in a way that he had never done before. Papa fully realized that this was a video and audio testimony that was of historical importance. His testimony was slippery without being vague, and he let Eric guide him into answering questions while denying absolute firsthand knowledge. In retrospect, if this was the best we could do then we had achieved a lot. This was E. Howard Hunt on camera talking about the JFK conspiracy. He cleverly substantiated what he had revealed in his taped "death-bed" confession in January 2004. The tapes are a historically significant document and contain hours of fascinating information. After the JFK portion was finished, we all breathed a sigh of relief. After a hearty lunch, we resumed our interview and moved on to many interesting topics about Watergate, prison life, and the current state of the CIA. All in all, there are about nine hours of tape.

Chapter Fourteen

American Spy:
A Story Of Betrayal

The book, *American Spy*, that was published shortly after my father passed away was the direct result of everything that Eric Hamburg and I had labored hard and long to achieve. After we flew back to California, Eric went to work putting a proposal together, with an outline of chapters and content for my dad's approval. At the same time he contacted his agent to begin finding a publisher. My father enthusiastically signed off on the first outline Eric sent him. Based on that, Eric wrote up a further proposal and gave it to his agent for circulation among publishers. Initially, our prospects looked really good.

This was to be the definitive life story of one of our nation's most infamous intelligence operatives. Unlike his first autobiography, *Undercover: Memoirs of an American Secret Agent*, which was quickly taken off the shelves in 1975 for glaring untruths, this was to be the real story. The main selling point of the book was, of course, new revelations by a key insider about the conspiracy to kill JFK . Finally, after forty-plus years, someone with real firsthand knowledge was coming forward to blow the whistle; naming names and con-firming that JFK had been killed as the result of a conspiracy within the American government.

Eric and I had signed a contract with my father splitting any profits from the book equally three ways. It seemed to be going smoothly, until Eric started getting phone calls from my father's attorney, Bill Snyder, and a bigger buffoon there could not be. This man had represented my father since Watergate and had even been recommended to him by William F. Buckley, Jr.

Snyder was real trouble for the project, and it's easy to speculate that he was more of a "handler" than a real attorney. A handler, in intelligence jargon, is someone who keeps a potentially embarrassing person in line. Eric and I suspected that Snyder was my father's handler for the CIA, and would go to any lengths to derail this project. Eric started getting phone calls and e-mails from Snyder protesting the nature of the revelations in the book proposal. When Eric countered that Papa had already approved everything, Snyder blew his top and threatened legal action against Eric and the publishers. He then sent a revised (censored) proposal, which excluded any reference to JFK other than to say that Mr. Hunt had no knowledge of any plot to kill Kennedy. It might as well have been written by one of the staff at Langley. This, of course, was unacceptable to us, and the shadow play went on for months, back and forth, revision after revision until there was nothing left of any real value in the book.

Snyder pressured my father into terminating our original contract for equal profits, and badgered him into signing a letter which said that I was not to discuss any part of the book with anyone, including Eric Hamburg, and my share was reduced to a mere 7%. The Miami Mafia prevented me from speaking with my father on the phone, and I found myself on the outside looking in. I couldn't believe this was happening. Snyder had successfully driven a wedge between us. He had secured the complete support of the self-serving second family that surrounded my dad with a miasma of fear and loathing; and kept him from doing what he had said he wanted. On top of all that, they had convinced my sisters that I had brow-beaten my poor father into making wholly untrue statements regarding the JFK assassination. I wrote a final plea to my father, not for the reinstatement of our original profit agreement, only asking that he retract cruel statements he had made in the letter to me.

I pleaded for a chance to prove that the charges Snyder had convinced him to make against me were completely false. Among those charges it was alleged that I had used his good name to borrow and/or steal money from his friends and associates. This was a ridiculous charge. I had never borrowed or accepted money from any person connected to my father. As a matter of fact, I never borrow money. This was clearly a campaign by Snyder and the rest to discredit me, and destroy our relationship. Why were they so afraid of me? Why did they feel so threatened? Was it really just because once these revelations came out, their precious little perfect lives would be soiled? The fact that I wasn't allowed to speak to him and that I lived so far away caused me a great deal of agony. Still, despite the hurt and bitterness, I didn't blame my father. They were the ones brow-beating him, and he was just too old and tired to resist them. In a final letter, the last one I ever got from Papa, he called for a truce. He said, "I'm too old and sick to fight with anyone, especially you, my first-born son. Let's just say that there have been too many things to forgive and too many to forget. Papa."

Snyder was now in total control of the woefully compromised project. Eric eventually backed out, saying that he could not be party to a book that was not truthful and would cast doubt on his reputation. The publishers were ready to back out of the agreement, saying, quite rightly, that there was no reason to go forward if my father was not going to disclose the JFK information. The point was also made that since Eric's departure from the project, the book had no author. My father was way too sick to write it himself, and it had always been understood that Eric would be the main author, with my father reserving final approval of the manuscript. Eventually, they found a new writer for the project, changed the title from *Final Secrets* to *American Spy*, and published it.

My father did not live to see its publication. He died in January 2007, about a month before the book came out. It received no critical acclaim, and was regarded as nothing of importance. Snyder and the family had won the battle, trivializing the book and gagging my father's last testimony. For me the greatest sadness was that I was never able to really speak to my father again. He died, and we never regained the love, trust and camaraderie that we had shared. After everything that happened in our lives, overcoming political issues, death, family loss, prison, drugs, it was tragic that Snyder and the Miami family had come between us. I blame them and, sadly, will probably never forgive them.

Chapter Fifteen

The Death Of E. Howard Hunt

The last time I saw Papa was in January 2007, when I flew to Miami a week before he passed away. The tension was as thick as the humidity when I arrived at my father's home in Miami Shores. The family's welcome was at best thin and superficial, but I didn't let that bother me; I was there for my father. He was barely recognizable when I walked quietly into his bedroom. The caregiver told me he hadn't been out of bed for a month. He spent most of his time sleeping, and Laura had finally agreed to get him a caregiver/housemaid while she was at work. Papa was sleeping as I pulled up a chair and sat next to his bed. His face was shrunken, especially because he wasn't wearing his teeth. He never adjusted to having dentures and he seemed just as happy without them. My father accepted his decline with frank dignity. He never allowed his physical problems to alter the fact that, even at his advanced age, he was a man's man. He had lived his life the way he wanted, he had endured hardship, and no one could say that he lived with-

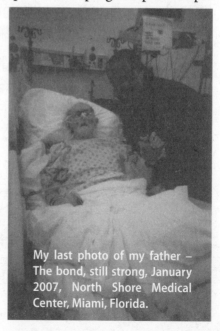

My last photo of my father – The bond, still strong, January 2007, North Shore Medical Center, Miami, Florida.

out personal loss or sacrifice. He had been betrayed by his government and his colleagues, and in the end, after all of the humiliation in the press, all the speculations and accusations, he still carried himself with grace and pride. I spent the next four hours sitting there, reflecting on our lives. There was so much to forgive, so much to embrace; it was utterly overwhelming.

Laura came home and gently woke him. "Howard, look who's here."

"Do you know who this is? Howard," she called, "do you know who this is?" Papa looked around the room as if in a trance and, looking me squarely in the eye, he said softly, "It's Saint, it's my son, Saint John." I looked into his eyes, searching for some special sign that all was forgiven. I needed to be forgiven, even if I had to do it on his terms. Everything had always seemed to be on his terms, so why should I think it would be any different now? Papa was the center of our family universe; Mama had been the gift, the work, the binding and the sorrow.

He raised his feeble hand, small as a child's. I gripped it, and poured my heart and soul, my love and devotion into him through our grasp. He held it tightly. His grip outlasted mine. He said nothing with words but he said a lifetime with his eyes; those steely, unflinching eyes, that could pierce through all the layers of self-protection; that could uplift you or reduce you to nothing. I spent my life hating and loving those eyes. He held my hand tightly for at least 10 minutes. Laura came back in the room and felt his forehead; it was hot. "He's got a fever," she said. "Maybe we should call 911."

"I don't think his fever is unnatural Laura, it's just his body saying it's time to go."

"Well you don't realize just how many times he's pulled through," she countered.

"What were Papa's wishes about his death?" I asked.

"Well, he doesn't want any major life support, and doesn't want to be fed through a tube or have his breathing maintained by a respirator."

"Don't you think he needs to die here in his home?" She ignored me and mumbled that she was calling 911. I had the fleeting thought of putting a pillow over his head and ending it all right there. I visualized myself in the act of suffocating my father, and wondered if my actions would result in a murder charge. Could they tell if I smothered my father? I didn't know. Instead of committing parricide, I got up and followed Laura out to the back porch. "Laura, I think he's trying to die. Do you really think he'll pull through this time?"

She looked at me in disbelief and said, "Saint, I just couldn't live with myself if I didn't give your father every opportunity to get better."

"I can tell in my gut, Laura, that he wants to die here at home, with us by his side. Don't take that from him."

"Saint, I know you love your father, but we've gone through this before, and he's pulled out of it. I'm sorry you're here to see all this."

"Sorry? I'm not sorry," I said heatedly. "I'm sorry for a few things but I'm not sorry that I want my father to die in peace. Just let him go," I pleaded, as she picked up the phone and made the 911 call.

"The ambulance will be here in a few minutes; do you want to ride with me or your father?"

"I'll ride with Papa."

There was nothing to do now, no arguing my point. Laura was his wife, and she had the power to do what she thought best. As I returned to my father's bedside, I wondered why she was seemingly unable to accept that he was really dying, and what superhuman strength compelled him to hang on. I whispered to him, "You can let go, Papa. It's going to be all right." Soon I heard the siren and in a few moments the medics were moving my father out the front door and into the ambulance. "I'm riding with him, I'm his son," I said. Papa seemed barely aware of what was going on around him. One ambulance trip melted into another and another and bright lights, nurses, prodding, and questions. All this, the wonders of modern medicine and free ambulance rides.

Papa on assignment, Vienna.
He would meet Dorothy here.

Chapter Sixteen

From My Eulogy For
E. Howard Hunt

A man is not only measured by his accomplishments, of which my father had so many, but also by the challenges he faced and how he dealt with them. My father's greatest challenge was not to allow overwhelming personal and professional tragedy to force him to live in anger and regret. My father met that challenge, and won. He showed me that in an ever-changing world of shifting values, his values are still the ones that count the most.

When I was born in 1954, my father was a young man of thirty-six. He had graduated from Brown University and survived World War II. He was well into his writing career, which would culminate in the publishing of his eighty-fifth novel, and third memoir next month. With one tour of duty as a naval officer under his belt, he joined the fledgling OSS. Never one to shy from hazardous duty, he made his reputation as a man who was skilled in both overt and covert duties. Papa had that rare combination of traits, which allowed him to be in the front lines of the action, and then, after changing into his Brooks Brothers suit, sit and have lunch with the Director of the CIA. He was the classic CIA man: an American James Bond. He had a sophisticated intellect, a taste for fine wine, good cigars, and international intrigue.

Deeply patriotic, he felt it was his calling to protect freedom and democracy at a time when much of the world was on the brink of Communist control. This did not come without a price: while trying to raise a family, the very nature of his work caused us to live like gypsies. True, we were exposed to the benefits of world travel and varied cultures, but we lacked a real sense of stability and security that only comes from growing up in the same familiar area.

I remember that by the time I was twelve, I had lived in Japan, South America, Mexico, Spain, France, and the U.S. I was raised speaking Japanese, and when we moved to Uruguay, I was faced with learning Spanish while attending a French school; thank you, Papa.

One of the most difficult times in my father's life was dealing with the aftermath of the Bay of Pigs operation. My father had been instrumental in merging the various anti-Castro Cuban Revolutionary groups and was something of a legendary figure known as "Eduardo." He viewed his Cuban brothers in arms as family, and was deeply committed to doing everything in his power to get them back to a free Havana. The fact that he had been betrayed by politicians whose only concern was their popularity was only a hint of what was to happen in later years.

I won't dwell here on the topic of Watergate except to say that for him and our family it was more than a national scandal; it was a personal tragedy and a nightmare that touched our lives with unforgiving brutality. My personal feeling is that my father's deep sense of loyalty and patriotism for this country was exploited by men of petty concerns and vastly inferior moral fiber.

I have some wonderful memories of my father: when I was just a toddler he would allow me to ride on his back as he crawled on all fours and made elephant sounds while I screamed with delight. In Japan he held me protectively while we swam, and at times, with mischievous intent, he left me standing in waist-high water while he nipped at my heels. He was a lover of jazz and was a gifted piano and trumpet player. During holidays and celebrations we would gather around while he sang and played songs on the piano, in awe of this complex man. For all his seriousness and unapproachability, he had a sweet playful side and a great sense of humor. His laugh was robust and house-shaking. Right up to the very end when he was slipping away, he displayed his humor by raising his hands into claws, just the way he did when he chased me around the floor so many years before.

He introduced me to jazz and showed me that he could play Harry James' trumpet solo in the classic Benny Goodman swing tune, "Sing, Sing, Sing." In the early 1970's when I was still under age he often took me to his favorite Georgetown jazz club called Blues Alley. He introduced me to Gene Krupa, Jimmy Rushing, and his close friend guitarist Steve Jordan. He shared his love of the outdoors with me, and I accompanied him on many hunting and fishing trips.

I remember well that horrible night in 1972 when he returned home after his men had been arrested at the Watergate. Alone at home with him, he simply said, "Son, I need your help." Of course, I was there for him.

Although in the years that followed we spent less time together, we never doubted the bond we had. We looked beyond our differences and loved each other unconditionally. When he moved to Guadalajara, he made me feel welcome at his home. Just because he was no longer a covert operative, didn't mean he stopped thinking like one. Here is one story I'll relate.

Desiring nothing more than a peaceful and idyllic life, he retired every night to bed and waited for sleep to take its restful hold. This was not to be! The neighbor had acquired a prize rooster and kept it on the roof. Every morning before the crack of dawn, that rooster would crow and shriek! As time went on, my father thought he would go mad. To remedy the situation he devised a plot to rid the world of that "devil rooster." He mixed some chicken feed and rat poison with water and froze it in an ice cube tray. After waiting for the neighbors to go to sleep, my father quietly slipped up to the roof, and using a sling shot, fired the poisoned ice cubes at the rooster. When the ice melted, the rooster fed, and, well, that was the end of that problem.

In the last few years he shared precious moments with me, and we often went out on walks; he was in his motorized scooter, while I walked at his side. He'd put on his old fishing cap, and we would patrol the neighborhood: the old spy and his son.

He had the great fortune of falling in love, marrying, and having families with not one, but two extraordinary women: Dorothy and Laura. Without the love and devotion of these two remarkable persons, there wouldn't have been any balance in his life. They were the glue that held us all together. They calmed him when he was angry, and soothed him when he was worried. They gave him wonderful children and filled his life with love and meaning. I've never seen anyone so devoted, so loving and caring as Laura was to my Papa.

The last time I saw my father was just days before he died. His grip was strong, and his eyes were clear. He faced the last days of his life with unflinching bravery and dignity: a warrior, a fighter and my hero till the end.

Chapter Seventeen

BREAKING THE STORY

I had started trying several months before he died to find another way to break the incredible information my father had given me. One of my old high school friends worked as a writer at *Rolling Stone* and after countless attempts to reach him, he finally returned my e-mail. To make a long story a bit shorter, I told him what I had and, after getting approval from his bosses, he flew to Eureka for three days of interviews. He examined all the documents I had, listened to the tape, and questioned me exhaustively. In the meantime the news broke that E. Howard Hunt had passed away, and it was all over the papers and the Internet. Eureka's newspaper, the *Times Standard*, sent someone over to cover the story from a local perspective. During that interview I let it slip that there might be a big story coming out with *Rolling Stone* magazine. Immediately I got calls from members of my family. I got calls from Snyder, the lawyer, whom I had hoped and prayed would not continue to be involved in family matters. This was not to be. There was no doubt that he was going to fight me every step of the way.

When the *Rolling Stone* article came out in April of 2007, the fecal matter really hit the fan! I got a call from the family saying they never wanted to talk to me again. As far as they were concerned I was no longer a part of the Hunt family. I had betrayed them and they considered me a lowlife. Immediately parts of the story were up all over the Net, and myriads of people had opinions

and set up websites to break the news that Hunt gave a "death-bed confession" with startling revelations naming the assassins of JFK. "Death-bed confession" was not a term I ever used. The title of the *Rolling Stone* article was, "The Last Confession of E. Howard Hunt," but, true to human nature, people went with the sexier "death-bed" thing, and it exploded into a media frenzy. I started getting calls from radio shows and decided to go ahead with interviews on some of the top programs.

I picked "Coast to Coast" with Ian Punnett, and he became the first to broadcast the taped confession my father made and sent to me back in 2004. Shortly before the airing, my sister Kevan called Ian and said that there was no such confession tape, that it was all a lie. Ian told her she should remain on the phone and tune in to the program. He said, "I've heard this tape now a dozen times and I assure you that this is nothing short of astounding." The problem my family had was that they didn't know Papa had made the tape, let alone its contents; so when it was broadcast it completely shut them up. To me, it was a major victory. I gleefully imagined Kevan's jaw dropping ... even becoming dislocated! The rest of the doubters never said another thing to me. What could they say? How could they deny words from the man himself?

I don't know what, if any, strategy meetings the family had to contain the story and destroy my character, but there did appear a "Hunt family" website with a long letter full of character assassination against yours truly. In it they brought up my drug use and claimed I had pressured an old and sick Hunt into making up false stories. I was a liar and shouldn't be believed. The response from the public was nearly unanimous: I was the bearer of truth. They were the liars and should be ashamed of themselves! Letters and e-mails started pouring in from all over the world thanking me for coming forward with the story.

With all the public support, I could bring the truth to a larger audience and agreed to go on the Alex Jones radio show. I had never heard of Alex, but I quickly learned that this was a man I could relate to. He was a freedom fighter in the purest

Good friend and truthseeker, Alex Jones.

sense of the word. An inexhaustible mover and shaker, he runs around like a six-headed demon attacking fraud and political corruption from every angle. He's a very controversial figure with a huge radio audience. My interviews on his show were a big success and we became good friends. His knowledge of the underside of political intrigue and misinformation is encyclopedic. Alex is a great supporter of mine, and I hope I am of him as well.

I did some smaller shows ... pirate radio and such, trying to reach as many people as I could. It was not only time consuming, but emotionally exhausting as well. Talking about my mother's death and answering questions about my past sometimes left me without the energy to get up from my chair.

The next media offer that came in was from *Inside Edition*, a Hollywood/News tabloid TV show. They wanted to put me on the air. I flew down to Los Angeles and met my friend Eric Hamburg. We had agreed to do the show together. We drove to their studios in Hollywood and waited for them to call us in for the taping. I had never done TV before and I didn't know what was going to happen. As I waited there the thought did occur to me that I might be getting a bad deal. What if the interviewer, Jim Moret, was working to discredit me? In a few moments I would know. My fears proved unfounded. Moret was not only a very nice man; he was an exceptional interviewer. He was smooth and direct without being abrupt. He handled me perfectly and we taped for about an hour. The final cut was much shorter of course, but it was very well received. After the show, Eric and I got a chance to hang out together.

There was a lot going on in my life and I was getting tired of the radio shows. I felt like I was getting repetitive and people were asking some pretty strange questions. One caller asked if I knew where JFK's brain was! Other people asked if Lee Harvey Oswald ever came to my house. Radio shows are very time consuming. You have to wait on the phone for long periods while the host does his advertising spots and talks to his other guests, who all have something to sell. It might be a DVD or a book, but they all have some kind of product.

I decided to bring something to the sales table. I went ahead and had an interview filmed, which I offered on a website that was created for me. On the website, you could hear the entire audio of my dad's "confession" and see a transcript of his words. There was also a link to sell my DVD. Was it wrong or unethical? It certainly was not. At best, what little money came in would barely offset the cost of manufacturing the DVD's and setting up the website. Unfortunately, by the time my DVD was available, I had tired of the radio shows and decided that Alex's would be the last for a while.

My father had instructed me to come forward with his revelations after his death and I felt like I had done a pretty good job. I had other things going on in my life. My wife, Mona Arnold, was the woman I had waited my entire life to meet. We met at College of the Redwoods, and I knew almost immediately that I would ask her to marry me. I decided to propose to her at the big Relay for Life cancer fund-raiser.

Chapter Eighteen

AFTERMATH

A couple of curious things happened to me just after the *Rolling Stone* article appeared. There was a break-in at the house where I had been renting a room, and a few days after that, someone tried to run me off a very dark and deserted road. I didn't see anything very sinister or conspiratorial about either incident, but some friends who know people that might know these things warned me about my safety.

The break-in at the house left no traces of entry and all the usual stuff people steal was untouched. There was stereo equipment, CDs, computers, DVDs, TVs, and nothing was touched. The only evidence was that whoever did it was looking for some papers. All of the files had been gone through. What were they looking for? It could have been the documents and memos that my father gave me outlining the plot to kill Kennedy, or it could have been ... I don't know what to think. Does this kind of thing actually happen in the real world? Do spooks break into people's homes? Was Dick Nixon tricky? Then again, wouldn't professionals have made it look like a normal robbery by a drug fiend?

Two nights later I was driving down Samoa Blvd., out by the dunes next to Humboldt Bay. It's a dark stretch of sandy windswept two-lane blacktop with no streetlights to speak of. It was late and I was returning to my house from my girlfriend Mona's apartment in Arcata. There was nobody else on the road when I noticed some headlights coming up fast behind me. As they got closer and closer I sped up a little, but they pulled back. They were about ten or more car lengths behind me when they sped up again. They came up so fast, right up to my bumper with their hi-beams on, that I swerved to avoid a collision. My car almost flipped on the sandy soil near the dunes.

The car sped past me and disappeared into the night. It scared me.

Mona and I got married on October 13, 2007, in a beautiful ceremony in Willow Creek, California. My brother David and his daughter were in attendance along with many of my best and dearest friends. I've had to let all of the controversy go; I felt it could easily take over my life. I want to be a "normal" person. My life has been crazy and dramatic, I've traveled all over the world, I know what people want and I've found it. It's not fame, drugs or money (although working for a living has its rewards); it's inner peace. People still stop me on the street and thank me for what I've done. I still get plenty of e-mails from people all over the world thanking me for coming forward with these tantalizing pieces of the puzzle. Little by little, some have come forward with enticing bits of information: like the guy who, now in his advanced years, saw my website and reached out to tell me that in 1963 he worked for the CIA stationed in Miami at the Opa Loka air base. He was a contract agent and a pilot. He knew my father and says that he flew him to Dallas in 1963. I've checked this guy out with Eric Hamburg and his story is credible.

Other people have found their courage and come forward with other bits of the story. One such person is Douglas Caddy. Doug Caddy was my father's first attorney during Watergate. He had also been the attorney for Billy Sol Estes. Estes is an interesting figure in the underbelly of Texas politics. He worked with Lyndon Johnson on various crooked land and water deals. He also claims that he was one of LBJ's closest confidantes. This is undisputed. That he carried out many shady and illegal activities on behalf of Johnson there is also little dispute. He has gone on record that LBJ told him (Estes) that he had been part of the plot to kill Kennedy. Doug Caddy sent me an e-mail encouraging me to continue fighting for the truth. Caddy also sent me an interesting DVD about LBJ's involvement in the murder of JFK. Caddy told me I was on the right track and that Estes had told him so.

Along with all the public support I've received, there has been evidence of pressure on the media not to play up the story. *60 Minutes*, the famous investigative show on CBS, called and wanted to flesh out a meeting with me in San Francisco. I phoned Eric Hamburg and we agreed to meet one of their top producers. I brought down all of the memos and tapes that I had in support of my father's story and had several good meetings with this producer, who shall remain unnamed. He was intrigued and excited about bringing this story to a national news audience with a ten-minute segment on an upcoming broadcast. He examined all the documents and we supplied handwriting experts to verify that the handwriting on the JFK memos was in fact that of E. Howard Hunt.

He flew back to New York and I went back to Eureka and waited. He called me the next week and said his boss had approved the story in a meeting that afternoon. Would I be willing to fly to New York to tape the interview? Wow! This was really big! Another week passed, and he called me again; this time with bad news. "As much as I wanted to run with this story, and I think it's a very important one, Saint John, I've been shut down."

"Shut down, what does that mean?" I asked.

"Well, I can't go into details but it came down from the top," he said. "What I'm supposed to tell you is that all of our time slots are booked till the fall season, so we'll have to get back to this later."

It's clear that this important story has been overlooked by the major news media because the powers that control them put their time and money into books and shows that support the lone gunman theory. Just look at two widely acclaimed books: *Case Closed*, by Victor Posner and the lengthy *Reclaiming History*, by ex-crime solver Vincent Bugliosi. That book is 1600+ pages thick and weighs a ton.

Bugliosi was asked on a radio show what he thought of the revelations coming from Saint John Hunt. He replied, "Well, you know, Saint John isn't credible." Mr. Bugliosi, you've cleverly slipped by the point. It's not my credibility you need to judge, I'm only the messenger. Call my father a liar if you don't believe his undisputed personal statements, made when he knew the end was near, but don't shift the burden of proof onto me. You can't say that my father's own words aren't at least worthy of further investigation. I have his memos and his tapes, and he gave me the task of bringing this to the world. There are still surprises left for people like Posner, *60 Minutes* and Bugliosi.

Ale x Jones, along with IFC (Independent Film Channel) flew Mona and me down to Dallas in January 2008 to be filmed for two documentaries about JFK's death. New witnesses have come forward as a result of my story and I was given the opportunity to tell my story on two films intended for a broad audience.

Being in Dallas at Dealey Plaza was very strange. I walked up the grassy knoll to the picket fence from which the fatal head-shot was fired. I went back to the railroad yard where police picked up the "tramps" and brought them into custody, only to let them go without establishing their identity. My father's role as a "benchwarmer" may never be fully disclosed. I knew that he was downplaying his involvement when he started writing the memos. We both knew he wasn't ready yet to tell the whole story. And now he never will. I'm left with parts of a puzzle.

Chapter Nineteen

THE CONSPIRACY

I've been asked many times what role I think my father really played in the killing of JFK. I have, of course, thought about it for a long time. After all the bits and scraps of information that I've been sent, careful examination of my father's notes and my own research into who the conspirators were and what connections they may have had, I have come up with what I believe to be a plausible scenario:

According to my father, LBJ and just about everybody else in the military-industrial complex viewed Kennedy as a threat and wanted him out of the way. Johnson knew that if Kennedy served another term, he probably had no chance of succeeding to the presidential throne, so he was open to suggestions, and agreed to control the investigation and cover-up in return for his ticket to the Oval Office. J. Edgar Hoover and the Kennedy brothers had been virtually at war, with Hoover having the institutional edge and aligning himself with Johnson.

It is alleged that just prior to the assassination, LBJ and Hoover held a secret meeting witnessed by LBJ's mistress, Madeline Brown. Brown also has gone on record as being present when LBJ said, in a moment of anger, that he was "taking care" of Kennedy. Billy Sol Estes, close friend of LBJ, confided to his attorney, Douglas Caddy, that LBJ had told him he was part of the move to kill Kennedy. I think in trying to find the right men for the job, LBJ landed on Cord Meyer. He was a CIA officer with international connections via London and was married to Mary Meyer, a socialite and mistress of Kennedy. She was later murdered on a Georgetown pathway, her home ransacked and her diary stolen, allegedly by James Angleton, chief of counterespionage for the CIA. LBJ must have known that Meyer had an ax to grind with Kennedy and wanted revenge.

From here the plot (according to my father) branches out to involve David Atlee Phillips, a close friend of my father and suspected handler of Oswald in Mexico City. Bill Harvey, another CIA officer, had been involved in many of the darkest ops in the CIA/Mafia plots against Castro. He was someone who wouldn't get squeamish about killing the President of the United States. In Harvey's biography there are notes and cables by Harvey discussing the need to recruit assassins from the Corsican underworld. Harvey was the one with the connections to do just that, and it was my father's contention that Harvey brought in Lucien Sarti as the hit man on the grassy knoll. Harvey was hoping his reward would be head of the CIA, after Johnson took control.

My father would have been the perfect man to organize the Cuban end of the assassination. Well known and respected in the underworld of anti-Castro Cuban exiles with revenge on their minds, he played the role of CIA link to these bloodthirsty mercenaries. Ever loyal to his bosses at CIA, my father shared their fear that Kennedy would virtually disband the CIA. Kennedy did in fact threaten to do just that. In addition he had fired my father's mentors and patrons after the Bay of Pigs disaster, thereby ending his rise up the CIA ladder. After that, his credibility, like so many others, was ruined.

The Cuban paramilitary group included Antonio Veciana, ruthless leader of Alpha 66 and well-known Kennedy hater whose CIA handler was none other than David Atlee Phillips, and Frank Sturgis, another CIA mercenary and Bay of Pigs veteran (he would later work for my father during Watergate and spend time with him in Federal prison). Another member was David Morales, admitted CIA executioner, with a list of bodies dating back to 1954, when he and my father worked successfully to overthrow the Guatemalan government. I believe Morales was part of the ground team and was at the meetings with my father in which the murder was discussed. In later years, personal friends of his have come forward with tales of a drunken Morales admitting to his role in Kennedy's death.

Morales died mysteriously just before he was to testify before the House Select Committee on Assassinations in 1978. Lucien Sarti was the Corsican assassin who, dressed as a policeman, fired the fatal head shot from the grassy knoll. According to witnesses, he was flown out of Dallas the day of the assassination. My father was a sniper during his stint in the OSS and had expertise in positioning a hit team using triangulation fire. I think it's plausible that he may have been the one who scouted out the positions for the three-man sniper team at Dallas. He was flown into and out of Dallas by a pilot from the CIA station in Miami in 1963, according to whom it may well fit the timeline. Frank Sturgis and Morita Lorenz, CIA contract agent and mistress of Fidel Castro, have testified that my father was in Dallas on that day and met with them at a motel room, at which time he gave Sturgis an envelope full of cash. Lorenz was a CIA tart who was used in attempts to kill her lover Fidel.

So there it is. Of course it's only a theory, but it makes sense to me. It's not so massive and is pretty well contained. You have the men who do the killing, Oswald the fall guy, and the secret CIA team, with Hoover and Johnson controlling the investigation/cover-up. It's simple, really.

What is so important about the Kennedy assassination? It's the defining moment when the "shadow government" finally took control and started running this country like their personal business. They got away with murder. After that, the rest was easy.

I thank all the people who support my going public, and I respect those who don't. I urge others to bring forward even the smallest links of information, and I pity my family for such cowardly and disgraceful attempts to keep the truth from coming to light. Most of all, and with a deep sense of pride and respect, love and admiration, I want to thank my father, E. Howard Hunt, who, after living with the terrible truth for over forty years, had the courage to tell me some of his secrets.

Chapter Twenty

Watergate as Conspiracy within Conspiracy

So much has been written about Watergate, yet so much of what the public believes is incorrect. Having been personally involved in the scandal and helping my father with the cover-up did much to distance me from understanding its true nature. I don't profess to be an authority on the subject, but I will try to explain my interpretation of one of the biggest political downfalls in modern times.

What was Watergate? Simply put, Watergate was the name of an office complex and adjoining hotel in Washington D.C. In 1972, the Watergate office complex housed the headquarters of the Democratic National Committee. Watergate has also come to encompass a political scandal that eventually caused the resignation of President Richard Nixon. Laying the blame for the scandal at Nixon's door is one of the untruths that have become fact in the minds of most people. The DNC office was the target of a burglary for the purpose of planting eavesdropping devices on the phones of one or more of its inhabitants. This is not the whole truth. The burglary in progress that was disrupted by D.C. undercover police officers was only one task in a much larger plan approved by various White House officials and carried out by ex-CIA and Treasury Department agents and a small band of Cuban exiles.

The "story" goes something like this. Nixon, who had won the Presidency in 1968, was by 1971 approaching re-election. In June of 1971, the *New York Times* started publishing a secret history of the United States' involvement in the Vietnam

War. This might be considered the Wiki-Leaks of its time. The documents known as the Pentagon Papers were excerpts from the classified files of the Defense Dept. 46-volume report revealing outright lies and fabrications fed to the media and the American public regarding Vietnam. The country at the time was already a tinderbox of anti-war sentiments culminating in widespread college shutdowns and massive anti-war demonstrations. The very vocal protesters wanted an immediate withdrawal from Vietnam. From the President's point of view, it was a very delicate time when the United States could reach an honorable peace as long as the Viet Cong and their allies were convinced that we would never pull out and allow South Vietnam to fall under Communist rule. The publication of the Pentagon Papers showed that the United States had been falsely promising a winning strategy in an unwinnable war.

In answer to this internal leakage of classified documents to the *New York Times*, it was decided to put together a secret covert-ops team (the Plumbers, to stop the leaks; get it?) that could run independently of normal FBI, CIA, and Dept. of Defense channels. According to most accounts, to this end Charles Colson, special counsel to the President, called up CIA agent and fellow Brown alumnus E. Howard Hunt. This is another falsehood of my father's, designed to give the impression that Colson recruited him. The truth is that my father called Colson many times prior to their first meeting in hopes that Colson would hire him for work in the White House.

Hunt had just "retired" from the Agency and was employed as an advertising executive by the Robert R. Mullen Company. He supposedly jumped at the chance to continue serving his country in this very special capacity. This is yet another untruth fabricated by the CIA and Hunt to give the appearance that Hunt was a "free agent" without ties to CIA. After his signing on, a teammate was picked to work with Hunt. This was G. Gordon Liddy, ex-FBI and Treasury Dept., who had worked with Egil Krogh on narcotics matters. Krogh was an advisor in the White House and liaison to the FBI and the Bureau of

Narcotics and Dangerous Drugs. His name would surface later in regard to the death of my mother Dorothy. Another ex-CIA man was added to the mix in the person of James McCord. His forte was wiretapping and related security and counter-measures.

Liddy was asked to prepare a multi-faceted plan for intelligence gathering in order to stop the leaks to the *New York Times* and keep an eye on the Democrats. This operation was named the Gemstone Plan, with the following code words:

Ruby: infiltration of the Democratic camp.

Emerald: a "chase plane" to eavesdrop on the Democratic candidate's aircraft and buses when his entourage used radio telephones.

Quartz: microwave interception of telephone traffic.

Sapphire: the use of prostitutes to compromise Democrats aboard a houseboat fitted with video recorders, to be moored near the site of the Democratic National Convention in Miami, Florida.

Crystal: electronic surveillance.

Garnet: counter-demonstrations.

Turquoise: operations making use of the air-conditioning system at the Democrats' convention hall.

Topaz: photographing Democrats' documents in the course of Crystal emplacements.

Opal: four clandestine entries. The targets were the Washington headquarters of Senator Ed Muskie and Senator George McGovern, the Fontainebleau Hotel in Miami, and a "target of opportunity" to be determined at a later date.

There were also, according to Liddy in his book *Will*, a staff of professional killers for missions involving kidnapping, drugging and forcible deportation of anti-war leaders. This group of killers could, according to Liddy, account for twenty-two deaths, including two hanged from a beam in a garage. Liddy claimed that this information was given him by E. Howard Hunt. The Cubans on this team, all connected to the infamous failed Bay of Pigs invasion, were trained by the CIA in various forms of murder, bomb-making, espionage, interrogation, covert entry, and production of false documents. In the course of time, I met and grew to know and admire some of these men. To me, they were friends and war comrades of my father's, and I was impressed by their deep loyalty to each other. I didn't know at the time that these were some of the same mercenaries that took part (according to my father) in the plot to kill John F. Kennedy. The Gemstone Plan was never fully approved but some aspects of it were, like the break-in at Watergate.

All of these plans and diabolical schemes were triggered by the Pentagon Papers leaks ... or were they? My Father went down to recruit his Cuban team for White House black ops in April of 1971. The first "Plumbers" operation was still three months away. It wasn't until June 1971 that the *New York Times* started publishing the Pentagon Papers. How can it be that this was a White House-run op? It has always seemed strange that the Pentagon Papers were of such paranoid concern to Nixon. They referred to a time when Vietnam was a Kennedy-Johnson war, not a Nixon war.

One of the first tasks given to my father was to find a means to discredit the man who had leaked the Papers to the *Times*. His name was Daniel Ellsberg. According to Ellsberg, he had been a top secret Defense Dept. analyst who felt a moral duty to report the truth about America's involvement in Vietnam. In July 1971, my father sent a memo to Colson outlining the need to put together a psychological profile on Ellsberg: anything that could make him look bad, as well as obtaining his psychiatrist's private files. Plans were made for my father to assemble his Cuban team for a break-in at Ellsberg's psychiatrist's office. Without going into further detail about this break-in, it is enough to say that this was just the beginning. By June 1972 my father was deeply involved in many illegal activities for the White House.

But my father was a double agent. He confessed to me over dinner at his favorite Cuban eatery that he in fact never retired from the CIA, and that the whole time he was working for the

White House and reporting to them, he was secretly reporting all of his findings and activities to the CIA. With this revelation, some of the puzzle begins to make sense. His bogus retirement and employment at the Mullen Company was not the first time he had used this as a cover. According to Jim Hougan in *Secret Agenda*, Hunt also "retired" from the CIA in 1960. He was given fraudulent retirement papers during the Bay of Pigs. He "retired" again in 1965. This time the cover story was that my father had retired to write novels based on his years at CIA. It was feared that if the KGB studied my father's books they would be able to glean bits of information about CIA operations.

The truth was that the books were meant to give disinformation to the KGB. It's somewhat comical to think that serious attention would be paid by the KGB to a "disgruntled" CIA agent, hoping to find important operational secrets in his pulpy spy novels! My father wrote five books in this series under the name David St. John. In 1970 when my Father "retired" again from the Agency, he was hired to work as a consultant to the Robert Mullen & Co. advertising agency, which turned out to be a "brass plate" CIA front operation.

Now, when we come to understand that Hunt's retirement from the Agency was only to give deniability in his latest CIA mission, that he was still working and reporting back to the Agency, that Mullen & Co. was a front, and that it was Hunt himself who pressed Charles Colson time after time to bring him into the White House, we can see that "Watergate" was a conspiracy within a conspiracy. It was the CIA placing their "mole" in the White House. Hunt's repeated visits to CIA Headquarters to obtain false documents, speech-altering devices, wigs, and pocket litter for his work at the White House give credible support to this scenario.

The break-in at Watergate that we all heard about was actually the third at those offices. The first two occurred in May, and had been unsuccessful in terms of retrieving anything of value for their sponsors. I'll never forget that night in June when my father woke me out of a sound sleep. When the Cubans and James McCord were caught with their hands in the cookie jar, one of the burglars had my father's name in his phone book. Exposed and vulnerable, he didn't know which way to turn for help. Should he expect help from the White House? Would the CIA give him cover? Not a chance. His CIA masters had covered their tracks well, and would not be coming to the rescue. The Nixon administration would conspire to keep its involvement secret, and pay off my father for his silence. It was this action, recorded by Nixon himself, which would cause the President of the United States to resign.

One further piece of evidence regarding CIA involvement in Watergate: the supplier of the actual bugging devices used by McCord was a wireman named Michael Stevens. His company was Stevens Research Laboratories (SRL), headquartered in Chicago. According to Stevens, McCord came to see him in May to place orders for bugging equipment. According to a Mr. Robert Barcal of Electronic Specialty Devices, SRL was a supplier of sophisticated electronic eavesdropping devices for the CIA. He testified that he was shown documents from the CIA giving SRL authorization to manufacture such devices. For a more in-depth look at this, please refer to Jim Hougan's book *Secret Agenda*. The importance of this became clear when my Mother's plane crashed in Chicago in December of 1972. She was supposedly carrying money to invest with cousins who owned a hotel.

After the plane crash and the headlines about Dorothy Hunt's death and the money, Stevens called the FBI and told them his life had been threatened and he believed that Mrs. Hunt had been murdered. He said that Mrs. Hunt was in fact on her way to pay him money to maintain his silence. Silence about what? Stevens says that he supplied McCord with the bugging equipment in May 1972 because McCord claimed he was engaged in an operation for the CIA. Stevens reported to investigators that the devices that he was working on for McCord were set to transmit over secret CIA frequencies, and able to transmit to the highly classified CIA, DIA, and NSA networks. Keeping this secret was why Mrs. Hunt flew to Chicago.

This conspiracy within a conspiracy unraveled and led to the death of my mother, the imprisoning of my father, the destruction of my family, and the loss of confidence that the American People oncehad for their government. Watergate touched us all; some, like me, more than others.

Fabian Ba

E. HOWARD HUNT
AND THE JFK PLOTTERS

by Eric Hamburg

How much of Howard Hunt's scenario holds up under examination? Surprisingly, a great deal. The men he names as part of the plot have cropped up over and over again in the assassination literature. There is substantial supporting evidence to implicate them in a plot to kill JFK. For this reason, Hunt's revelations are more credible than they might otherwise be. A review of the literature indicates why this is so.

Let's start with William Harvey. Hunt, who called Harvey an "alcoholic psycho," named him as the master planner of the plot. There is ample evidence for both of these propositions.

Consider the following statements regarding Bill Harvey, made by author Anthony Summers in his seminal work, *Conspiracy*. Summers writes, "In the closing stages of the [House] Assassinations Committee mandate, some staff members felt that, while Mafia marksmen may have carried out the assassination, it could only have been orchestrated by someone in American intelligence, someone with special knowledge of Oswald's background. As they pondered this, investigators gave renewed attention to the senior CIA officer who co-coordinated the CIA-Mafia plots against Castro – William Harvey."

Summers goes on to state, "William Harvey died in 1976 ... As far back as 1959, he was one of only three officers privy to plans to send false defectors to the Soviet Union. 1959 was the year of Oswald's suspect defection. Genuine defection or not, Harvey almost certainly knew about it in detail.

"Subsequently, Harvey was the man who conceived and planned the CIA's Executive Action program, the contingency plan for foreign assassinations. He was in close touch with men of the same ilk as Lucien Sarti, and the Corsicans now alleged to have been the gunmen in Dealey Plaza.

"Next, as head of Task Force W, Harvey was in direct charge of anti-Castro operations, in personal touch with the mobsters Santos Trafficante and John Roselli, inciting them to murder Fidel Castro. He became a close friend to Roselli."

Harvey hated Bobby Kennedy with a "purple passion," and the feeling was mutual. He sent commando teams into Cuba at the height of the missile crisis in 1962, which made Bobby Kennedy furious. As a result, Bobby had Harvey transferred out of Washington and sent to the CIA's station in Rome, Italy.

Summers adds, "Yet Harvey was still meeting with Roselli, in the United States, as late as June 1963, and I have learned that he visited anti-Castro camps in Florida, at a time when he was theoretically already in Rome. According to new, unresearched information, initial approaches to hire assassins in Europe were made in Rome – sometime before the recruitment approaches allegedly made to the Corsican Mafia in Marseilles."

Summers quotes one Assassination Committee staffer as saying this: "The feeling of some of the CIA people we talked with was that Harvey was heavily involved with the organized crime figures. The feeling was that he was out of control and may have worked with organized crime figures to murder JFK. He behaved as if he was all-powerful ... He may have been the key to accomplishing the assassination."

This staffer was probably Dan Hardway, a member of the professional staff of the House Select Committee on Assassinations, which investigated the Kennedy assassination for the US Congress in the late 1970s. In his book *Flawed Patriot*, author Bayard Stockton quotes Hardway as saying this of Harvey: "I had placed him in the middle of a web of intrigue. Harvey was central to everything that went on ... Harvey was a natural suspect. He had the assassination teams. He was in charge of JM/WAVE [the CIA station in Miami]. I was convinced that Bill Harvey was involved in the assassination. I wanted to investigate Harvey vigorously ... I was determined to prove his complicity in the assassination, if I could."

Bill Harvey had a history with the Corsican Mafia. In her book *ZR Rifle*, Claudia Furiati wrote, "It was learned that during 1961, William Harvey traveled to Marseille in France and recruited another agent (code name QJ/WIN) who worked on the Lumumba case. WIN appears in the House Committee investigations: he was one of the men from the Corse Union, the Marseille organized crime group, which showed the presence of the Mafia in the plans to assassinate foreign leaders. QJ/WIN met the indispensable requirement of being a Mafioso of non-U.S. origin."

Various versions of QJ/WIN's identity have been published, but it is interesting to note his connection to Marseille and the Corsican Mafia. QJ/WIN was recruited by Harvey as a possible assassin or recruiter of assassins for the CIA, along with another mysterious figure code named WI/ROGUE. Both men were sent to the Congo to take part in a plot against Congolese leader Patrice Lumumba, who was indeed assassinated in January 1961, just before Kennedy took office.

Harvey had an affinity for Corsicans, particularly for use in assassination operations. In *Flawed Patriot*, former CIA officer Bayard Stockton writes that Harvey recommended Corsicans for use in the ZR/RIFLE assassination program. "According to the one set of notes available, Harvey's inquiries during his trip to Europe seemed to center on Trieste ... ZR/RIFLE was intended to be carried out by non-American criminal elements." In his memo, Harvey wrote, "Exclude organized criminals, e.g. Sicilians, criminals, those w/ record of arrests, those w/ instability of purpose as criminals." But he added, "organization criminals, those with record of arrests, those who have engaged in several types of crime. Corsicans recommended. Sicilians could lead to Mafia."

Stockton also suggests that Harvey may have used his time in Rome to recruit European criminals for the JFK plot. "Once in Rome, Harvey might have contacted European criminals and/or the Union Corse [Corsican Mafia] , the Sicilian Mafia [with whom he had loose liaison], and the mainland Italian Camorra [Mafia], on behalf of Roselli. Thus, though it has not been proved, Harvey may have acted as a line of communication between European and American plotters." He adds, "Harvey left behind a hint that he had some knowledge of the JFK killing. After he had testified to the U.S. Senate's Church Committee in 1975, he commented, 'They didn't ask the right questions,' implying that he might have had some answers to more pointed questions regarding the assassination."

"Corsicans recommended." Harvey gave the same advice to Peter Wright, head of British intelligence, who wrote about this in his memoir *Spy Catcher*. Biographer Bayard Stockton, an old friend and colleague from Harvey's days in Berlin in the 1950s, ultimately reached the conclusion that Harvey was not involved in the assassination, despite the overwhelming evidence against him. Stockton justifies his conclusion with this blanket statement: "No one who knew Harvey at his prime believes, or believed that he possibly could have been involved in the JFK assassination. No one. Not even those who had reason to dislike him."

But that statement is false. Its validity flew out the window when E. Howard Hunt, who knew Harvey and worked with him in the CIA, asserted his strong belief that Harvey was the prime mover behind the assassination. Stockton, who died shortly after his book was published in 2006, could not have known that, even as he was writing those words, they were being contradicted by the words of E. Howard Hunt.

In his memoir *American Spy*, posthumously published in 2007, E. Howard Hunt said this of Bill Harvey: "There has been suggestion in some circles that CIA agent Bill Harvey had something to do with the murder and had recruited several Corsicans, including a crack shot named Lucien Sarti, to back up Oswald and make sure the hit was successful. Supposedly, Sarti was dressed in a Dallas police uniform and fired the fatal bullet from the grassy knoll behind the picket fence ... Is it possible that Bill Harvey might have recruited a Mafia criminal to administer the magic bullet? I think it's possible ... Harvey could definitely be a person of interest, as he was a strange character hiding a mass of hidden aggression. Allegations have been made that he transported weapons to Dallas. Certainly it is an area that deserves further investigation."

Hunt goes on to say of Harvey's role in the plot, "If that's the case, Harvey had seniority and would have been the person in charge, with the others taking orders from him ... Having been stationed in Rome, he very well might have come into contact with the Corsican Mafia and heroin traffickers whom theorists claim he recruited for the assassination ... Harvey, however, is the most likely suspect. If he felt his position was in jeopardy, he was the type of person who would have taken drastic action to remedy the situation. It is a big leap, because he was a brain-addled pistol-toting drunk ... but there is the slightest possibility that Harvey and LBJ could have formed some kind of thieves' pact between them."

Hunt adds, "If LBJ had anything to do with the operation, he would have used Harvey, because he was available and corrupt ... Who knows the depth of Harvey's criminal connections? He may easily have known Mafia members who have been named as possible conspirators, such as Johnny Roselli, Santos Trafficante, Sam Giancana, and Carlos Marcello ... These are names which have come up in connection with the assassination plot on Castro."

So much for Stockton's assertions of Harvey's innocence and his pristine character references.

All of these quotes are taken directly from videotaped interviews that I conducted with Howard Hunt in Miami, April

2005, along with his son St. John. Hunt also mentioned another suspicious CIA figure, David Morales, in connection with Bill Harvey: "Another CIA person of interest who has been linked to that dreadful day is David Morales. Bill Harvey posted Morales to the CIA's Miami station in 1961, where he became chief of Covert Operations for JM/WAVE, an operation to destabilize Castro after the Bay of Pigs. Morales and Harvey could have been manufactured from the same cloth – both were hard-drinking, tough guys, possibly completely amoral. Morales was rumored to be a cold-blooded killer, the go-to guy in black ops situations where the government needed to have someone neutralized. I tried to cut short any contact with him, as he wore thin very quickly."

Clearly, Bill Harvey is a highly suspicious figure in any scenario. But could Harvey have done all this on his own? When I met with Fabian Escalante, former head of Cuban intelligence, in Havana in 1994, he expressed skepticism. "Harvey had to have a patron," he said, "and that patron was Richard Helms." Helms was the CIA's Deputy Director for Plans (head of its covert operations division) in 1963, and later became Director of the CIA under President Johnson. Helms was close to Harvey, and also to Howard Hunt. But Helms was a very discreet figure who kept his hands clean.

In *ZR Rifle*, Claudia Furiati describes Helms this way: "And who was the author of the entire scheme? Richard Helms, the brain of the CIA. Helms was the ultimate chief of the covert and parallel operations from the beginning of Operation Mongoose [the CIA's plot to kill Castro]. He was the director of the plans which included the [poison] capsules, the special missions, the terrorist commandos, the Mafia, the Banister unit, Pontchartrain, William Harvey, Manuel Artime, Rolando Cubela, Desmond Fitzgerald, Lee Harvey Oswald, Santos Trafficante, David Atlee Phillips, and ZR Rifle. He was the conductor of the invisible government and the maestro of plausible denial. Finally, he was the link of the Agency with the 'hardliners' and the mentor of the provocations during the Kennedy administration. But Helms' involvement was not apparent; he was behind four walls, an invisible man."

Furiati, writing before Helms' death in 2002, described him this way: "Currently he is a business consultant. He is tall, with fine black thinning hair. He is discreet and evasive; the perfect bureaucrat. He is considered the most astute and the coldest of all the directors of the Agency – so cold that he was nicknamed "Mr. Cool."

Mr. Cool – an invisible man, hidden behind four walls. What an apt description of Richard Helms. Howard Hunt, in *American Spy*, put it this way: "But in the end, Helms was an expert in CYA (cover your ass), not CIA. When the time came when he might have been able to help me and come to my defense, Dick said, 'Oh, Hunt ... Oh, well, I sort of know him. He was a romantic.' And that was all he had to say about me. He pretended that he barely knew me when in fact he had known me for years."

Hunt related to me a very interesting anecdote about Helms and LBJ, which he included in his book. He wrote, "During the course of a year, we would have lunch between three and six times. In fact, Helms had made a confidant out of me, once calling me at the office to say, 'Meet me downstairs right away. I have something to tell you.' What he had to tell me was that he had broken up with his wife and had moved to a country club in anticipation of a divorce. This was, at the time, extremely privileged information. We had lunch about six weeks later. Helms told me that he had just been summoned down to LBJ's ranch and had spent a wild weekend there riding a jeep at top speed through the property. Out of that emerged the confidence that he was going to be announced as the deputy director of the CIA, which, of course, evolved over time to DCI [Director of Central Intelligence, to which he was appointed by Johnson]. So far as I know, I was the first person he told about such important events in his life."

But why did LBJ summon Helms to his ranch, when he could have easily informed him of this in Washington. Could it be that at this meeting, LBJ flashed a green light to Helms for a plot against JFK, in the privacy of his own Texas ranch? This can only be speculation, but it is clear that Helms had a good and close relationship with LBJ. This meeting had to have taken place in late 1961 or early 1962, as Helms was appointed Deputy Director in February of 1962. And as Hunt points out in his book, "LBJ appointed him as director, but he wouldn't play ball with Nixon or comply with Nixon's requests to investigate White House leaks, so the president [Nixon] basically fired him, sending him to Iran during Watergate."

In his own posthumous memoir, *A Look over My Shoulder*, Richard Helms wrote this of his relationship with Johnson and Nixon: "I was never sure why President Nixon distrusted me, aside from associating me with Allen Dulles and the other East Coast, Ivy League, establishment figures whom he loathed and thought of as dominating the upper brackets of OSS and subsequently CIA. In contrast, I always had an excellent relationship with Lyndon Johnson, who had at least as much claim as Nixon to have been born in a log cabin, and whose views of Ivy Leaguers were, at the best, reserved."

Obviously, Helms and Johnson were close. Likewise, Helms and Hunt were close for many years. Hunt never claimed that he himself had any direct contacts with LBJ. So if Hunt believed that LBJ was involved in the plot to assassinate JFK, which he clearly did, his impression probably came via Richard Helms, the missing link between LBJ and Howard Hunt. Helms was also the missing link between LBJ and Bill Harvey.

And what of Richard Nixon? In his interviews with me, Howard Hunt was adamant that Nixon had no role in the JFK assassination. Hunt wrote in *American Spy*, "As far as I'm concerned, as paranoid as he was, Nixon would never have been involved. He would not only have been horrified of the action but would never have trusted anyone to know he was involved." Hunt seemed to me to be sincere in this belief, although he did not say the same of Lyndon Johnson.

On the famous "smoking gun" Watergate tape of June 23, 1972, Richard Nixon said this to his top aide H.R. Haldeman: "When you get in there with Helms, say, Look the problem here is that this will open the whole Bay of Pigs thing ... It would be very bad to have this fellow [E. Howard] Hunt, he knows too damned much.... It would make the CIA look bad, and it's likely to blow the whole Bay of Pigs thing, which we think would be most unfortunate – both for the CIA and for the country."

H.R. Haldeman, in his memoir *The Ends of Power*, offered his interpretation of this statement. He wrote, "It seems that in all of those Nixon references to the Bay of Pigs, he was actually referring to the Kennedy assassination ... After Kennedy was killed, the CIA launched a fantastic cover-up ... In a chilling parallel to their cover-up at Watergate, the CIA literally erased any connection between Kennedy's assassination and the CIA ... And when Nixon said, 'It's likely to blow the whole Bay of Pigs thing', he might have been reminding [CIA Director] Helms, not so gently, of the cover-up of the CIA assassination attempts on the hero of the Bay of Pigs, Fidel Castro – a CIA operation that may have triggered the Kennedy tragedy and which Helms desperately wanted to hide."

This is highly suggestive, to say the least. Haldeman in his memoir also quoted former Senator Howard Baker, a member of the Senate Watergate Committee, as saying, "Helms and Nixon have so much on each other that neither one of them can breathe." Perhaps Helms was blackmailing Nixon with his knowledge that Tricky Dick had originated the assassination plots against Castro (with the help of E. Howard Hunt), plots that may have morphed into a plot against JFK. And Nixon might have been blackmailing Helms with his knowledge of the CIA's role in the JFK plot. In any case, Nixon found it expedient to get rid of Helms at the height of Watergate, removing him from the directorship of the CIA and dispatching him far away as U.S. ambassador to Iran. It is still an open question as to what Nixon meant when he said on the tapes, "This fellow Hunt, he knows too much." It is also unclear what Nixon was referring to when he said, "We protected Helms from one hell of a lot of things."

In his own memoir, *RN*, Nixon wrote that he was never able to get the CIA's complete file on the Bay of Pigs, despite repeated requests to Helms. Nixon compared the CIA to a locked safe, to which he could never get the combination. This might have been an additional factor in his decision to remove Richard Helms as DCI.

Could LBJ have flashed a "green light" to Richard Helms during their private trip to the ranch? The idea is not unprecedented. Historian Arthur Schlesinger has suggested, in his book *Robert Kennedy and His Times*, that then-Vice President Richard Nixon may have given a similar signal with regard to the assassination plots against Fidel Castro as far back as 1960. Schlesinger wrote, "Yet the [assassination] plan was an integral part of the invasion plan. And it is hard to suppose that even the runaway agency mordantly portrayed in the reports of the President's Board of Consultants would have decided entirely on its own to kill the chief of a neighboring country. [CIA Director] Dulles must have glimpsed a green light somewhere. Could it have been flashed by the Vice President of the United States? 'I have been,' Richard Nixon said in 1964 of the invasion project, 'the strongest and most persistent advocate for setting up and supporting such a program.'"

Similarly, presidential historian Michael Beschloss wrote in his book *The Crisis Years*, "We will probably never know for certain whether Vice President Nixon flashed the green light for a CIA-Mafia attempt against Castro. But it is hard to believe that as President he would have made such a heavy-handed demand of Ehrlichman merely to retrieve evidence of his support for invading Cuba in 1960 ... The demand makes more sense if Nixon was worried about public embarrassment by information showing his involvement in a murder plot against a foreign leader. This concern may have led to Watergate."

These are two highly reputable historians both suggesting that Nixon may have given a "green light" to assassination plots against Castro. Granted, Nixon was not Johnson, and Castro was not JFK. But the same principle applies. And if we assume that there is a straight line connecting the CIA-Mafia plots against Castro to the plot against JFK, then surely there is a similarity in the modus operandi of the two plots. Nixon would naturally not want his connection to the plot exposed, yet his tacit approval may have been necessary for the plot to go forward. Likewise, LBJ's flash of a green light to Helms may have provided him with all the authority necessary to go forward with the plot against JFK. In both cases, we have means, motive and opportunity, but we do not have definitive proof. And such proof may be impossible to find, given the extreme secrecy and sensitivity of these operations. We can only speculate, and wonder.

But E. Howard Hunt clearly believed that LBJ was part of the plot. In *American Spy*, Hunt wrote this: "Lyndon Johnson was an opportunist who would not have hesitated to get rid of any obstacles in his way. He could easily have been in touch with [Bill] Harvey or [David] Phillips ... Phillips was a man on the way up and became a significant figure that LBJ would have wanted to get to know ... In Washington there is a caste system in regard to who will talk to whom. Would LBJ have spoken directly to Harvey? Yes, I think he could have done that, as Harvey's rank and position was such that a vice president could talk to him. Harvey may have had an intense personal dislike for the Kennedys and even had a severe clash with Bobby Kennedy around the time of the missile crisis."

Hunt went on to add, "The person who had the most to gain from Kennedy's assassination was LBJ. There was nobody with the leverage that LBJ had, no competitor at all. He was the vice president, and if he wanted to get rid of the president, he had the ability to do so by corrupting different people in the CIA. It has also been said by many LBJ biographers, such as Robert Caro in *The Path to Power*, that the man idolized money, was corrupt and unprincipled, with unlimited ambition – not the type of individual who was content to end his career as vice president ... Many people conjecture that Johnson was set to drop even lower in footnote status, observing that he was set to be cut from the 1964 presidential ticket. He and Kennedy did not get along, and theirs was purely a marriage of convenience ..."

Hunt concluded that, "Having Kennedy liquidated, thus elevating himself to the presidency without having to work for it himself, could have been a very tempting and logical move on Johnson's part. It wouldn't have been hard for him to make contact with Harvey, another ruthless man who was not satisfied with his position in the CIA and its government salary. He definitely had dreams of becoming DCI, and LBJ could do that for him if he were president. If LBJ had anything to do with the operation, he would have used Harvey, because he was available and corrupt. LBJ had the money and the connections to manipulate the scenario in Dallas and is on record as having convinced JFK to make the appearance in the first place." Of course, we know that LBJ did not make Harvey the DCI [head of the CIA], but rather put Richard Helms into this position – perhaps another indication that Helms was a key figure in the plot.

And what do we know about Lucien Sarti, the French Corsican Mafia gunman named by Howard Hunt as the second shooter on the grassy knoll? In a sidebar to the *Rolling Stone* article entitled "The Last Confession of E. Howard Hunt," writer Rob Sheffield wrote, "A Corsican drug trafficker, Sarti was killed by police in 1972. Conveniently, nothing concrete is known about him." But this is not true. In his book *The Great Heroin Coup*, published in 1980 before Sarti's name was connected with the JFK assassination, Heinrik Kruger detailed aspects of Sarti's criminal career. In his preface to the book, noted JFK researcher Peter Dale Scott states, "... as support for his argument that the traffic once dominated by Ricord was simply redirected to Cuban exiles in touch with the CIA and with Santos Trafficante, Kruger points to the extraordinary story of Alberto Sicilia Falcon. Somehow Sicilia, a twenty-nine year-old

Cuban exile from Miami, was able to emerge as the ringleader of the so-called 'Mexican connection' which promptly filled the vacuum created by the destruction of the Ricord network in 1972. Lucien Sarti, a top Ricord lieutenant, was shot and killed by authorities in Mexico on 27 April 1972, after being located there by U.S. agents." This latter fact is quite interesting. Eliminating international drug traffickers was one of the missions of the White House plumbers unit, of which Hunt was a member, and Sarti's murder occurred just before the Watergate break-in in June 1972. Is this a link between the JFK assassination and Watergate – or is it just another coincidence?

Speaking further of the Ricord drug organization in France, Kruger writes this: "The Ricord organization was divided into four teams ... Ricord himself ran the main team from Asuncion, Paraguay, and oversaw the entire operation. Chiappe and Michel Nicoli led another team, Dominique Orsini and Louis Bonsignour a third, and Andre Condemine and Lucien Sarti a fourth.... It was Murder Incorporated in French. Nearly all had been sentenced to death in France." It is interesting to note the inclusion of the name Michel Nicoli, who later became one of those who identified Lucien Sarti as the shooter of JFK, while Nicoli was in the federal witness protection program in the US.

Kruger refers again to Sarti in his book, saying, "In 1966 Old Man Ricord enlarged his already immense narcotics network upon discovering how easily he could smuggle heroin into the US via Latin America ... The old man surrounded himself with hardcore thugs. By 1970 the Mob's leaders were Ricord, sentenced to death in absentia for treason, torture and murder; Lucien Sarti, wanted for the murder of a Belgian policeman; Christian David, sentenced to death in absentia ... and French gangster and former SAC agent, Michel Nicoli." Nicoli and Christian David, of course, were later the two French criminals who independently identified Lucien Sarti as the assassin of JFK, in separate confessions to author and investigator Steve Rivele.

Kruger further details the hunting down and death of Lucien Sarti. He says that, "Auguste Ricord's 1971 imprisonment in

Paraguay taught Christian David and Lucien Sarti that it was time to move on. Their choice of location was Brazil, in particular Ilha Bella, an island off the coast north of Santos, conveniently only two hours from Sao Paulo and five from Rio de Janeiro. It also provided a small harbor and landing strip. The two holed up in the Bordelao, a small hotel run by Haide Arantez and Claudio Rodriguez, friends of Sarti's Brazilian mistress, Helena Ferreira. Beau Serge [Christian David] was by then the undisputed boss of the 'Brazilian Connection.' Its other leaders were Sarti, Michel Nicoli and several others."

Kruger describes the event's leading to Sarti's death. "In March Sarti went to Mexico City, where he was joined by his wife Liliane in an attractive residential district apartment. Sarti had no notion that the police had been trailing him ever since his entry into Mexico. Somebody had tipped them off ... In the evening of April 17, Sarti and Liliane left their hideout to go to the movies. Before they got to their car, they were surrounded by the police. Sarti was unarmed, but the police shot and killed him, and arrested Liliane."

In their book, *Marseille Mafia*, Pierre Galante and Louis Sapin provide further background on Sarti's criminal career. In 1961, Lucien Sarti was involved in the murder of a Belgian police constable named Albert de Leener. The officer was ambushed by a group of French criminals, one of whom was Sarti. De Leener was shot and killed, and his body dumped into the trunk of a car. "The body was lifted up; the boot of the car opened. During the operation, a small piece of cardboard fell from the pocket of the man who had fired the final shot. The investigators found it on the pavement, a little later. It was a fake identity card bearing the name Lucien Sabatier. The photo was of a known French criminal, aged about thirty, who had a record under that name at the Quai des Orvefres. He was called Lucien Sarti.

"The following evening, arriving in Paris, Lucien Sarti read the papers and learned that he had been identified ... He was now a hunted man. There was only one thing for him to do: go to South America." His trail from there led him to Mexico, and from there on to Dallas, according to the findings of author Steve Rivele.

In 1985, Rivele became interested in the Kennedy assassination and in particular the French connection. Rivele was a successful author who later became a prominent screenwriter in Hollywood. Rivele's research led him to a man named Christian David, who had been a prominent member of the French connection, and a leader of the Corsican Mafia. He was then serving time in Leavenworth Penitentiary. Rivele helped David find an attorney, and in return was told a remarkable story by David.

As recounted in the book *Conspiracy*, by Anthony Summers, "In May or June 1963, according to David, he was asked by Antoine Guerini, the Corsican Mafia boss in Marseille, to accept a contract to kill 'a highly placed American politician.' Guerini made it obvious whom he meant, calling the politician 'le plus grosse legume' – the biggest vegetable. The President was to be killed on US territory. David turned down the contract, on the ground that it was too dangerous.

"The contract, said David, was accepted by Lucien Sarti, a Corsican drug trafficker and killer, and two other members of the Marseille mob, whom he refused to name. They were, he said, 'specialists de tir' – 'sharpshooters.' He learned what happened some time after the assassination, at a 1965 meeting in Buenos Aires. Present were Sarti, Michel Nicoli, [Christian] David and two others. This is how the assassination was carried out, as David tells it."

Rivele described the scenario, which he learned independently from both Christian David and Michel Nicoli, to British journalist Anthony Summers. In *Conspiracy*, Summers writes, "Sarti and the two other assassins flew from Marseilles to Mexico City in the fall of 1963. They stayed there several weeks, and were then driven to the United States border, which they crossed at Brownsville, Texas. They were met at the border by a representative of the Chicago Mafia, who conversed with them in Italian. [Could this have been Johnny Roselli?] He drove them to a house in Dallas."

Summers goes on to add, "On November 22, David told Rivele, three gunmen were in position. Two were in buildings to the rear of the President when he was hit – one of them 'almost on the horizontal.' The third killer, Sarti, dressed in some sort of uniform as a disguise, was 'on the little hill to the front, the one with the fence.' Four shots were fired that day, according to Sarti and another of the assassins. The first shot, from the rear, struck President Kennedy in the back. The second shot missed, and hit 'the other man in the car' [Governor John Connally]. The third shot, from Sarti on the hill, struck the President in the head, killing him. Sarti used 'an explosive bullet,' the only member of the group to use that type of ammunition. The fourth shot missed the car entirely."

This scenario is remarkable in that its details fit so well with evidence developed by the House Select Committee on Assassinations and other sources. But there is more. "After the assassination, according to David's allegations, the murderers lay low in Dallas for about two weeks. Then, says David – 'they were then flown out of the country by private aircraft, to Montreal.'"

This is the story of the assassination, as relayed from Christian David to Steve Rivele to Anthony Summers. When Rivele asked David who could confirm his story, he named Michel Nicoli, a fellow Corsican gangster who was then in the U.S. federal witness protection program as a result of his 1972 testimony against the mob. A DEA official who knew him vouched for his credibility in strong terms. Eventually, Nicoli was located, and he told Rivele the same story that David had told, although the two men had not seen each other for years. The FBI did nothing to follow up on this remarkable development.

In his account of the conspiracy, E. Howard Hunt named eight central figures. These were Lyndon Johnson, Cord Meyer, David Atlee Phillips, William K. Harvey, Antonio Veciana, Frank

Sturgis, David Morales, and Lucien Sarti. Of these, perhaps the most surprising name is that of Cord Meyer. Meyer was a high official of the CIA, who had good reason to hate John F. Kennedy, yet his name has rarely come up in assassination circles.

Cord Meyer was born in 1920 and graduated from Yale in 1942. He joined the US Marines and served in the South Pacific, losing an eye in combat. In 1945, he married Mary Pinchot, who would later have an affair with President Kennedy. In 1947, he was elected president of the United World Federalist, and was a strong left-wing advocate of world government and the United Nations.

However, by 1949, Meyer had joined the CIA at the urging of Allen Dulles and worked closely with James Angleton, among others. Meyer's views gradually moved from left to right, and he became a strong anti-Communist, as well as a heavy drinker. In 1958, he was divorced from Mary Meyer, who was a free-spirited artist. In 1961, Mary began an affair with President Kennedy, which lasted until his death (she had known him as far back as prep school in the 1930s). In 1964, Mary was murdered mysteriously during an evening stroll on the banks of the towpath in Georgetown. Officially, the murder was never solved, although rumors had it that the CIA might have been involved. Shortly after her death, James Angleton of the CIA broke into her studio and retrieved her personal diary, the contents of which have never been revealed. Cord Meyer left the CIA in 1977, and died in 2001.

In my conversations with Howard Hunt, it was clear that he was fascinated by both Cord and Mary Meyer, in particular her mysterious death, just after the release of the Warren Commission report. This was also evident in his memoir, *American Spy*. Among other things, Hunt wrote, "Another name that pops up in JFK conspiracy theories is Cord Meyer. He was a high level CIA operative whose wife, journalist Mary Pinchot, was having an affair with John F Kennedy ... By the time of the assassination, Cord had been promoted to chief of the CIA's International Organizations Division ... The theorists suggest

Cord would have had a motive to kill Kennedy because his wife was having an affair with the President.... Then, on October 12, 1964, Mary was tragically gunned down while walking on a towpath in Georgetown. By that time, she and Cord had divorced, and the media did not realize that her former husband was a high-ranking CIA official. Neither did they find out about her relationship with the President ..."

Hunt went on to describe the suspicious circumstances behind Mary Meyer's death. "Mary had cautioned at least one close friend to grab her diary if anything ever happened to her. Journalist, later editor of the *Washington Post*, and Kennedy friend Ben Bradlee happened to be married to Mary's sister, Antoinette, who found the letter and diaries shortly after the death. But there is an interesting fact here. When the Bradlees arrived at Mary's house shortly after the murder, they found James Angleton already there, rummaging around the house, looking for the diary and letters ... Bradlee has said that the door was locked when he arrived. So does that mean Angleton broke in?"

It was clear to me from my conversations with Hunt years later that he was bitter about the fact that Angleton had broken in and gotten away Scot free, whereas Hunt himself had served 33 months in prison for a similar break-in. Hunt's theory of the break-in went like this: "When Antoinette eventually found the diary, she turned it over to Angleton, who later admitted that the book detailed the affair, talking specifically about how Mary and Kennedy would drop LSD before making love. Mary apparently thought that JFK's murder had taken place because the industrial-military complex couldn't allow his mind to be expanded by the drug. The fact that Angleton was already there in the house when Bradlee got there is mysterious, as so little time had gone by since the murder." Bear in mind that Angleton was a very high official of the CIA, unlikely to personally take part in a "black bag job" except in the most extreme circumstances. This would be roughly equivalent to J. Edgar Hoover personally breaking into a building on behalf of the FBI.

Hunt concluded his analysis with these suggestive comments: "Journalist Leo Damore wrote in the *New York Post* that a CIA source told him that Mary's death was probably a professional hit because 'She had access to the highest levels. She was involved in illegal drug activity.' What do you think it would do to the beatification of Kennedy if this woman said, 'It wasn't Camelot – it was Caligula's court?' So I think it was probably a professional hit by someone trying to protect the Kennedy legacy." Or was it, perhaps, to cover up her knowledge of the Kennedy assassination?

Renowned historian John H. Davis, author of several books on the Kennedys and the assassination, himself a cousin of Jacquelyn Bouvier Kennedy, wrote an unpublished manuscript in 1998 entitled "John F. Kennedy and Mary Pinchot Meyer: A Tale of Two Murdered Lovers." Wrote Davis, "When, in early October, 1964 Mary Meyer first read the Warren Report on the assassination of President Kennedy she immediately recognized it as a cover-up. Among its many omissions Mary noted there was no mention in the Report of the CIA-Mafia plots to assassinate Castro." She told a friend that the document was full of lies and that 'they had covered up everything.'"

Davis added, "We may picture this slim blonde woman of 44 in her small coach house studio in Georgetown ... leafing through this report on the murder of a man she had seen regularly during the last 20 months of his life, then tossing the book aside in disgust ... and phoning up a few of her closest friends to tell them she thought the Report was worthless, that it was full of glaring omissions and was essentially a 'pack of lies.'... If it became known among those who perpetrated the cover-up that some woman who had been close to President Kennedy was going around blabbing her mouth off about some of the most sensitive, and potentially explosive, omissions in the Report, that person was taking an enormous risk."

Davis concludes: "It was a tribute to the perspicacity of Mary Meyer to recognize at first reading what almost no one recognized at the time: that the Warren Commission's investigation of the JFK assassination was deeply flawed and that the official finding was essentially a fraudulent cover-up... We must inevitably conclude that Mary Meyer's rejection of the Warren Commission's conclusions when an entire nation was accepting them indicated that she knew things that very few people knew and that for that reason told Anne Truitt she feared for her safety and told her that if anything happened to her she should consign her diary to the CIA's James Jesus Angleton. The burning question, then, is what did Mary know? And the only answer we can give is that she knew too much."

In the book *The Georgetown Ladies' Social Club*, by C. David Heymann, Leo Damore was quoted as saying this: "Mary Meyer was killed by a well-trained professional hit man, very likely somebody connected to the CIA. After the assassination of John Kennedy, Mary had become an inconvenient woman, the former mistress of one of the world's most powerful political leaders and the ex-wife of a CIA honcho. The feeling in the Agency was that here's somebody who knows too much for her own good. She knows where all the bodies are buried. She knows the Warren Commission report, released shortly before her death, is nothing but a grandiose cover-up. She knows about the Mafia, the Cubans and the Agency, and how any one of them could have conspired to eliminate Kennedy. What she didn't know, according to Damore, is that a month after the President's murder, the Agency placed her under twenty-four hour surveillance, tapping her phone, wiring her house, intercepting her mail, and initiating several break-ins in search of notes and letters to and from JFK and others of equal interest."

Interviewed by author David Heymann shortly before his death in 2001, Cord Meyer was asked about the death of his wife Mary. "It was a bad time," he said. "And what could he say about Mary Meyer? Who had committed such a heinous crime?" His answer to Heymann was revealing. "'The same sons of bitches,' he hissed, 'that killed John F. Kennedy.'"

Another key figure in the plot, according to Hunt, was David Atlee Phillips. Phillips was a Latin American specialist who worked with Hunt on the CIA coup in Guatemala as far back as 1954. He also collaborated with Hunt on the plans for the Bay of Pigs invasion in 1961. The two men were close friends and collaborators over many years in the CIA. Author Gaeton Fonzi, who investigated Phillips in depth for the House Select Committee on Assassinations, came to some firm conclusions about David Phillips, who had allegedly met with co-conspirator Antonio Veciana, a Cuban exile leader, under the pseudonym Maurice Bishop, in the summer of 1963 in Dallas in the presence of Lee Harvey Oswald. The ostensible purpose was to put Oswald, who was about to travel to Mexico, in touch with Veciana's cousin Guillermo Ruiz, who worked in the Cuban embassy in Mexico City.

In his book *The Last Investigation*, Gaeton Fonzi wrote this: "'Maurice Bishop' was David Atlee Phillips. I state that unequivocally ... In addition to the abundance of evidence detailed in this book, which unerringly points to Phillips being Bishop, believe me, I know that he was. And Bob Blakey [staff director of the committee] and the House Select Committee knew that he was, although its report did not admit that."

Fonzi goes on to add, "David Atlee Phillips played a key role in the conspiracy to assassinate President Kennedy. I don't embrace the assumption that Phillips' relationship to Oswald may have been extraneous to any conspiratorial role."

It should be noted here that Howard Hunt insisted to me, and wrote in his last memoir, that Phillips met with Oswald not just in Dallas, but also in Mexico City, where Phillips was stationed.

Fonzi continues, "That Phillips rose to the top echelon of the Agency as Chief of the Western Hemisphere division is, I think, significant when we talk about 'elements' of the CIA being involved in the Kennedy assassination. (Can those who control the ideological soul and operational body of the Agency be considered simply 'elements' within it?)" It should be noted, though, that Richard Helms admitted he kept CIA Director John McCone in the dark about all assassination activities, so the plot probably did not go to the very top of the CIA hierarchy.

Gaeton Fonzi went on to add, "Nor is Phillips' tight working association with the Agency's most lethal operatives insignificant. His was a cabal of associates whose careers were entwined with the history of CIA assassination plots, that ranged from Richard Helms to E. Howard Hunt and from Ted Shackley to the Agency's Mob liaison William Harvey. And then, of course, there was David Phillips' faithful operative, the CIA's action legend, David Sanchez Morales, whose inebriated admission of involvement in the Kennedy assassination – 'We took care of that son of a bitch, didn't we?' – closed the circle."

Fonzi concludes, "I believe that David Atlee Phillips' key role was affirmed when he lied under oath. The very fact that he had to lie – both about his manipulation of Oswald in Mexico City and his covert operations as Maurice Bishop – was the definitive statement of his guilt." Significantly, Hunt admitted that Phillips had met with Oswald in Mexico City shortly before the assassination (presumably to frame him as a Cuban sympathizer), as well as in Dallas before his Mexico trip. It has also been reported by author Tad Szulc, in *Compulsive Spy*, that Howard Hunt was in Mexico City at the very time Oswald was visiting there. This raises the possibility that both Phillips and Hunt may have met with Oswald there. How else would Hunt know of the meeting with Phillips? In his interviews with me, Hunt did not deny that he was there at the same time as Oswald, but said he would have to check his CIA records.

What of Antonio Veciana? He was a Cuban exile, leader of the militant anti-Castro group Alpha 66, and apparently met with Lee Harvey Oswald and David Phillips prior to the assassination. In E. Howard Hunt's handwritten memo given to his son St. John prior to his death, Hunt wrote this: "1962 - LBJ recruits Cord Meyer. 1963 – Cord Meyer discusses a plot with Phillips, who brings in William Harvey and Antonio Veciana. He [Phillips] meets with Oswald in Mexico City that summer. Veciana meets with Frank Sturgis in Miami and enlists David

Morales in anticipation of killing JFK there. But LBJ changed the itinerary to Dallas, citing personal reasons." There is much more to Hunt's memo, but in this passage it is clear that Veciana was a key figure in the plot.

British author Anthony Summers, in *Conspiracy*, said this about Veciana: "Antonio Veciana was the victim of a murder attempt in late 1979 – an ambush while he was on his way home from work. Four shots were fired, and a fragment of one bullet lodged in Veciana's head. He recovered – in what police and doctors consider a freak escape. Publicly the veteran anti-Castro fighter has blamed the attack on Castro agents, but privately he has also expressed concern that it may have been linked to his allegations about CIA case officer 'Maurice Bishop', who – says Veciana – met Oswald shortly before the Kennedy assassination and later urged the fabrication of a false story about Oswald and Cuban diplomats in Mexico City."

Veciana, who later took part in a failed assassination attempt with David Phillips in 1971 against Fidel Castro in Chile, is clearly a very suspicious character. He is also the only one of the plotters named by Hunt who is still living. In a recent interview, Veciana told David Talbot, author of *Brothers*, that he believed the CIA was involved in Kennedy's murder. Predictably, Veciana denied that he himself had any part in the plot.

Another key figure in the plot was David Morales. In his handwritten memo, Howard Hunt wrote, "In Miami, Sturgis tells Hunt that he's buying guns for some friends (who could be Mafia or Cuban activists). Sturgis brings Morales to a meeting he has with NADA [Howard Hunt] where the 'Big Event' is referred to. After Morales leaves, Sturgis says 'Are you with us?' Hunt replies that he can't make a decision without knowing what the 'Big Event' is. When Sturgis says killing JFK, NADA [Hunt] is incredulous. Doesn't have a lot of faith in Sturgis and says, 'You guys have got everything you need – why do you need me?' Sturgis replies that NADA [Hunt] could help covering up. NADA [Hunt] says he won't get involved in anything involving Bill Harvey, who is an alcoholic psycho. That ends

121

NADA's [Hunt's] part. He resumes his normal life and does not see Sturgis again until [Bernard] Barker brings him into the Watergate break-in."

This passage contains many interesting elements. First, it is clear that Morales had prior knowledge of the "Big Event," having been brought into the plot by Veciana.

Second, it is evident that Morales had direct dealings with Veciana, David Phillips, Frank Sturgis, Howard Hunt, and possibly Cord Meyer as well. Morales had worked with Hunt and Phillips in the CIA coup in Guatemala as far back as 1954, as well as in the Bay of Pigs operation and the plots against Castro in the early 1960s. Morales was known as a stone killer and a field operative who was not afraid to get blood on his hands. He was reported to have been in the presidential palace in Chile when President Salvador Allende was assassinated in 1973, and also took part in the CIA Phoenix assassination program in Vietnam.

In Fonzi's book, he describes an incident that took place during a late night drinking bout with Morales and a friend named Bob Walton. "At the mention of Kennedy's name, he recalls, Morales literally almost hit the ceiling. He flew off the bed on that one," says Walton... He jumped up screaming, "That no good son of a bitch motherfucker! He started yelling about what a wimp Kennedy was and talking about how he had worked on the Bay of Pigs and how he had to watch all the men he had recruited and trained get wiped out because of Kennedy."

"Walton says Morales' tirade about Kennedy, fueled by righteous anger and high-proof booze went on for several minutes while he stomped around the room. Suddenly he stopped, sat back down on the bed and remained silent for a moment. Then, as if saying it only to himself, he added: 'Well, we took care of that son of a bitch, didn't we?'"

Now we come to Frank Sturgis. Sturgis was a mercenary and soldier of fortune, with ties to both the CIA and the Mafia. Sturgis had fought briefly on the side of Fidel Castro in the mountains during the revolution, then later switched sides and became violently anti-Castro. Fidel installed Sturgis for a short time as the Minister of Gaming (gambling) when he took power, but Sturgis was quickly removed when Castro closed the Mafia casinos and outlawed gambling in Cuba.

Sturgis was associated with Howard Hunt for many years, starting with a novel Hunt wrote in 1949 called *Bimini Run*, which featured a soldier of fortune named "Hank" Sturgis. (Hunt later maintained that this was just a coincidence.) Sturgis worked closely with Hunt during the Bay of Pigs period, and of course was later arrested with him over the Watergate break-in during 1972. Hunt claimed under oath that he had met Sturgis for the first time shortly before Watergate, but this was clearly not true, by his own later admission.

In her book *ZR Rifle*, Claudia Furiati points out some pertinent facts about Sturgis (aka Frank Fiorini). She writes, "The counter-intelligence – Frank Sturgis and Orlando Bosch were two of the principal agents of Operation 40, the 'parallel' counter-intelligence structure before, during, and after the Bay of Pigs invasion. David Atlee Phillips represented the CIA in these operations.

"The Commandos - Sturgis was one of the initiators of the International Anti-Communist Brigade ... David Atlee Phillips was the mentor of these terrorist groups. Sturgis and his partner Gerry Hemming opened the training camp at Lake Pontchartrain in New Orleans in the same era as the creation of Alpha 66 [headed by Antonio Veciana] ... Pontchartrain, spared by the police authorities, became the center of the illegal counterrevolutionary operations. Frank Sturgis, Orlando Bosch, Guy Banister, David Ferrie, Clay Shaw, and Lee Harvey Oswald all participated directly in these."

For her book, Claudia Furiati interviewed Fabian Escalante of Cuban intelligence, who in turn cited the book *Double Cross*, by Sam and Chuck Giancana. Escalante commented, "It is interesting to observe, following the details given in *Double Cross*, that the assassination of Kennedy was carried out by two groups: one under the control of Jack Ruby, who later killed Oswald; and the other by Frank Sturgis, who later became the chief of the Watergate 'plumbers'. It is now possible to appreciate why Richard Nixon didn't want the famous phone tapes about the Bay of Pigs to become known."

The "Bay of Pigs thing" raises its ugly head again. But why was Nixon so concerned about the Bay of Pigs thing, and what it might reveal. After all, the invasion took place under JFK, who took full responsibility for the fiasco. Why then would this cause such embarrassment to Nixon and to the CIA? Perhaps it was a result of the events leading up to the Bay of Pigs, the planning of which took place under Nixon and Eisenhower, and the aftermath of the failed invasion, which caused hatred toward Kennedy on the part of the CIA, the Cuban exiles, and the Mafia. Perhaps these three groups joined forces to plot the murder of JFK. And perhaps Nixon realized that the whole chain of events could be traced back to him, starting in 1960 with the plots against Castro. And who suggested such a plot? One of the first was none other than E. Howard Hunt.

As the planning for the Bay of Pigs progressed, Hunt became increasingly dissatisfied with the program being proposed. He felt that "his" Cubans were being pushed out in favor of more moderate to leftist Cuban exiles – in effect Fidelismo without Fidel. Shortly before the actual invasion, Hunt in effect resigned his position in the operation. In his book *Oswald and the CIA*, historian John Newman writes, "After a detour of several days in Spain, Hunt delivered his recommendations to the Cuban task force [headed by Nixon] in April. He listed four:

"Assassinate Castro before or coincident with the invasion (a task for Cuban patriots).

"Destroy the Cuban radio and television transmitters ...

"Destroy the island's microwave relay system ...

"Discard any thought of a popular uprising against Castro until the issue has already been militarily decided.

"Hunt believed that, without Castro, the Cuban army would 'collapse in leaderless confusion.' [Tracy] Barnes and

[Dick] Bissell read Hunt's report and told him it 'would weigh in the final planning.'"

Subsequently, in July 1960, Hunt was invited to lunch with Nixon's National Security Adviser and Chief of Staff, Robert E. Cushman. Newman, quoting Hunt himself, says, "Hunt described what transpired: 'I reviewed for Cushman my impressions of Cuba under Castro and my principal operational recommendations ... Cushman's reaction was to tell me that the Vice President [Nixon] was the project's action officer within the White House, and that Nixon wanted nothing to go wrong.'"

Of course, Nixon and Cushman were gone, and Kennedy was President, by the time the operation took place in April 1961. Why, then, Nixon's great concern, a decade later, about the "Bay of Pigs thing," and the fact that E. Howard Hunt "knew too much." Nixon told Ehrlichman that "if you open that scab [Hunt], there's one hell of a lot of things." What they were has never been revealed.

Clearly, though, Hunt knew or was familiar with many of the key plotters, as well as the plot itself. Hunt claimed in his memo that he turned down the invitation to play an active role, although he certainly did not alert the police, the FBI, the CIA, or the Secret Service. On an audio tape given by Hunt to St. John in his latter years, Hunt described himself as a "benchwarmer" in the plot to kill JFK. While this does not describe an active participant, it does describe a full member of the team who was ready to take the field at any moment if the need arose. Of course, Hunt could also have been minimizing his role, as might be expected of a career spook.

In his handwritten memo to St. John, Hunt added this: "Like the rest of the country, NADA [Hunt] is stunned by JFKs death and realizes how lucky he is not to have had a direct role. In Danbury federal prison [after Watergate], Epsilon [Sturgis] and NADA [Hunt] reflect on the 'Big Event.' Oswald is dead so the feds have nobody to prosecute. Epsilon [Sturgis] speculates that Jack Ruby was selected to kill Oswald by the mob. Epsilon [Sturgis] reveals that one of the Dallas shooters was a foreigner." Hunt later informed St. John and me that the foreigner was a French Corsican gunman named Sarti. This could only have been Lucien Sarti, as Hunt suggests in *American Spy*.

Clearly, Hunt was up to his eyeballs in assassination plots. One additional note is provided by Bayard Stockton in *Flawed Patriot*: "In March 1961, well before [Bill] Harvey was involved in Caribbean matters, [Johnny] Roselli went to the Dominican Republic, accompanied by Howard Hunt of the CIA. Rafael Trujillo, the Republic's dictator, was ambushed and killed on May 30, 1961, but the CIA was cleared of involvement in the assassination." Cleared by the CIA itself, that is, just as it was "cleared" of the assassination of Lumumba in the Congo in 1961, even though the Agency had sent killers to eliminate him.

It is most interesting to note that in 1961, two years before the Kennedy assassination, Howard Hunt and Johnny Roselli were joining forces in an assassination plot in the Caribbean. Roselli, of course, was the Mafia's liaison to the CIA, and the representative of the Chicago Mafia in Las Vegas, Los Angeles and points east. He was also a close friend and drinking buddy of Bill Harvey, and of David Morales as well.

When we put all these facts together, from various sources, it becomes clear that Howard Hunt's assassination scenario is at least very possible, if not highly probable. If Hunt had wanted to create a fictional scenario, he would more likely have implicated Fidel Castro and the "Communist Menace" in the plot, instead of his own close friends and colleagues. This adds considerably to the credibility of Hunt's story.

DOCUMENTS
&
PHOTOGRAPHS

E. Howard Hunt – Testament
to his son, Saint John Hunt

Recorded January 2004

I heard from Frank [Sturgis] that LBJ had designated Cord Meyer Jr. to undertake a larger organization while keeping it totally secret.

Cord Meyer himself was a rather favorite member of the Eastern aristocracy. He was a graduate of Yale University and had joined the Marine Corps during the war and lost an eye in the Pacific fighting.

I think that LBJ settled on Meyer as an opportunist (unintelligible) like himself (unintelligible) in a man who had very little left to him in life ever since JFK had taken Cords wife as one of his mistresses.

I would suggest that Cord Meyer welcomed the approach from LBJ who was after all only the Vice President at that time and of course could not number Cord Meyer among JFK's admirers; quite the contrary.

As for Dave Phillips, I knew him pretty well at one time. He worked for me during the Guatemala project. He made himself useful to the agency in Santiago, Chile where he was an American businessman. In any case, his actions, whatever they were, came to the attention of the Santiago Station Chief and when his resume became known to people in the Western Hemisphere Division he was brought in to work on Guatemalan operations.

Sturgis and Morales and people of that ilk, stayed in apartment houses during preparations for the big event. Their addresses were very subject to change so that where a fellow like Morales had been one day, you'd not necessarily associated with that address the following day. In short it was a very mobile experience.

Let me point out at this point, that if I wanted to fictionalize what went on in Miami and elsewhere during the run up for the big event, I would have done so.

But I don't want any unreality to tinge this particular story – or the information I should say. I was a benchwarmer on it and I had a reputation for honesty.

I think it's essential to refocus on what this information, that I've been providing you – and you alone by the way, consists of. What is important in the story is that we backtrack the chain of command up through Cord Meyer and laying the doings at the doorstep of LBJ.

He in my opinion, had an almost maniacal urge to become President. He regarded JFK, as – as he was in fact, an obstacle to achieving that. He could have waited for JFK to finish out his term and then undoubtedly a second term.

So that would have put LBJ at the head of a long list of people who were waiting for some change in the Executive Branch.

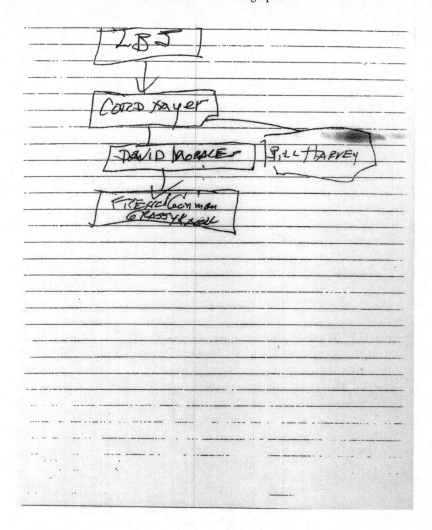

The "chain of command." Hand written memo by E. Howard Hunt give to me his son, Saint John Hunt.

1962

LBJ recruits Cord Meyer.

1963 Cord Meyer discusses a plot
with Philips and to bring
in Wm. Harvey and
Antonio Veciana. He meets with
Oswald in Mexico City that
summer.

Veciana meets w/ Frank Sturgis
in Miami and enlists David
Morales "in anticipation of killing
JFK there. But LBJ changes
itinerary to Dallas, citing personal
reasons.

In Miami Sturgis tells Hunt
that he's buying guns for some
friends (who could be Mafia or
Cuban activists). Sturgis brings
Morales to a meeting he has with
NADA where "The Big Event" is
referred to. After Morales leaves
Sturgis says, "are you with us?" Hunt
replies that he can't make a
decision without knowing what the
"Big Event" is. When Sturgis says
killing JFK, NADA is incredulous.
Doesn't have a lot of faith in
Sturgis and ~~says~~ "I never had

1962 LBJ recruits Cord Meyer

1963 Cord Meyer discusses plot with Phillips and he brings in Wm. Harvey and Antonio Veciana. He meets with Oswald in Mexico City that year.

Veciana meets w/ Frank Sturgis in Miami and enlists David Morales "in anticipation of killing JFK there. But LBJ changes itinerary to Dallas, citing personal reasons.

In Miami Sturgis tells Hunt that he's buying guns for some friends (who could be Mafia or Cuban activists). Sturgis brings Morales to a meeting he has with NADA [Hunt] where "The Big Event" is referred to. After Morales leaves Sturgis says, "Are you with us?" Hunt replies that he can't make a decision without knowing what "The Big Event" is. When Sturgis says killing JFK, NADA is incredulous. Doesn't have a lot of faith in Sturgis and says [you] had

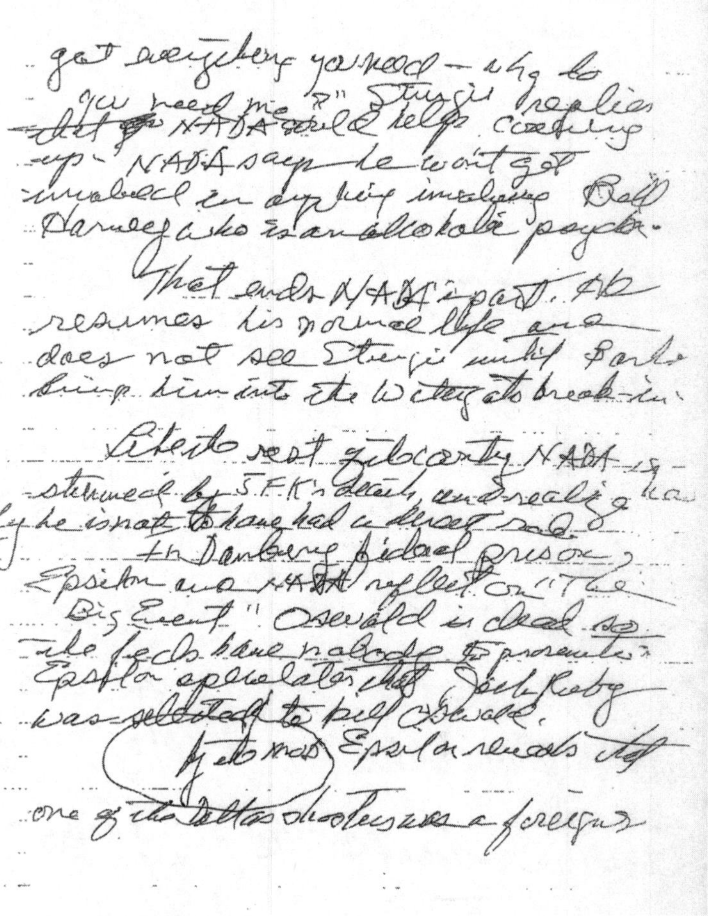
got everything you need — why do
you need me?" Sturgis realizes
NADA should help covering
up. NADA says he won't get
involved in anything involving Bill
Harvey who is an alcoholic psycho.

That ends NADA's part. He
resumes his normal life and
does not see Sturgis until Barker
brings him into the Watergate break-in.

Like the rest of the country NADA is
stunned by JFK's death, and realizes how
lucky he is not to have had a direct role.
In Danbury federal prison,
Epsilon and NADA reflect on "The
Big Event." Oswald is dead so
the feds have nobody to prosecute.
Epsilon speculates that Jack Ruby
was selected to kill Oswald.
(by the mob) Epsilon reveals that
one of the Dallas shooters was a foreigner

got everything you need – why do you need me? Sturgis realizes NADA should help covering up. NADA says he won't get involved in anything involving Bill Harvey who is an alcoholic psycho.

That ends NADA's part. He resumes normal life and does not see Sturgis until [Bernard] Barker brings him into the Watergate break-in.

Like the rest of the country, NADA is stunned by JFKs death and realizes how lucky he is not to have had a direct role. In Danbury federal prison [after Watergate], Epsilon [Sturgis] and NADA [Hunt] reflect on "The Big Event." Oswald is dead so the feds have nobody to prosecute. Epsilon speculates that Jack Ruby was selected to kill Oswald by the mob. Epsilon reveals that one of the Dallas shooters was a foreigner.

JFK — Alpha

C. Myers — BETA

M. " — Chi

Bill Harvey — Delta

F. Sturgis — Epsilon

J. Angleton — Phi

L.B.J. — NU

DAVID A. Philip — Sigma

Marita LORENZ — TAU

DALLAS — Omicron

Antonio Veciana — theta

DAVID Sanchez Morales — Gemini

Hunt — Nada

Barker — Aries

Danbury federal P.

In preparation for giving actor Kevin Costner enough information to begin negotiations, my father developed this code key.

1962

recruits

1963

- discusses a plot
with   a to bring
in   and
                   He meets with
Oswald in mexico City that
summer.
                meets a
in miami and /enlists.
              "in anticipation y killing
JFK there. But   a large
itinerary to Dallas, city passed
reasons.
   In miami   tells Hunt
that he's bringing 4 you /a some
friends (who are like Mafia or
Cuban activists).   bring
         to a meeting   with
HADA where "The Big Event" is
referred to. After   leaves
         says, "are you with us?" Hunt
replies that he can't make a
decision without knowing what the
"Big Event" is. when   says
killing JFK, HADA is incredulous.
Doesn't have a lot of faith in
and   "I knew him

Next two pages (147-148) – My father had me white out the names and replace with code
names.

137

get everything you need — why do
"you need me?" NASA replies coming
up — NASA says he won't get
involved in anything involving
who is an alcoholic psycho.

That ends NASA's part. He
resumes his normal life and
does not see until
bring him into the W city to break in.

Libeits rest of country NASA is
stunned by JFK's death, and realizes how
lucky he isn't to have had a drug sale
in Danbury federal prison.
Epsilon and NASA reflect on "The
Big Event." Oswald is dead so
he feels have nobody to prosecute.
Epsilon speculates that Jack Ruby
was selected to kill Oswald.
(by no one) Epsilon reveals that
one of the Dallas shooters was a foreign

Late 1962
"Nu" recruits "Beta"

1963
"Beta" discusses a plot with "Sigma" who brings in "Delta",
and "Theta".

"Theta" meets with Oswald in Mexico City that summer.

"Theta" meets with "Epsilon" in Miami, and enlists "Gemini" in
anticipation of killing Kennedy there.

"Nu", changes location of "The Big Event" to Dallas, Texas,
citing personal reasons.

In Miami, "Epsilon" tells "Nada" that he is buying guns for an op
code named "The Big Event"
"Epsilon" brings "Gemini" to a meeting with "Nada" in which
"The Big Event" is referred to.
After "Gemini" leaves, "Epsilon" says "are you with us?"
"Nada" replies that he can't make a decision without knowing
what "The Big Event" is.
When "Epsilon" says "killing Kennedy" "Nada" is incredulous.
"Nada" doesn't have a lot of faith in "Epsilon" and says "you
seem to have everything you need, why do you need me?"
"Epsilon" replies that "Nada" could help by lending credibility,
as well as aiding in the clean up.
"Nada" says he won't get involved in anything that involves
"Delta" because he is an alcoholic and a psycho.

"Nada" doesn't see "Epsilon" until many years later
In "D.F.P." "Nada", and "Epsilon" reflect on "The Big Event", and
"Epsilon" reveals that Oswald fired from the rear but the fatal
shot was fired by a pro from out of the country. The name of
this man was told to "Nada" by "Epsilon"

I typed this letter and sent it to Kevin Costner.

Additional hand written notes from E. Howard Hunt to me.

Cuba Project:

LBJ had most to gain from JFK's death. Morales & thousands of national Cuban exiles detest the Kennedys
LBJ's lifelong corruption makes him a logical.

Cord Meyers - head of Intel Division, then
COS Great Britain -
wife: Mary Meyers, Philadelphia socialite

Next two pages (151-152) - Additional background notes. This is revealing because my father had sworn in court testimony that he never knew Frank Sturgis until 1971. This proves that Hunt and Sturgis were well acquainted by the time of the JFK assassination.

Early in the Bay of Pigs operation Bernie Barker brought Frank Sturgis (nee Fiorini) to my safe house with a defected Cuban who had been chief of Castro's air force. They had overflown Havana and asked for gas money to repeat the leaflet flight. I scrapped together $500 but told them the USG's policy was against it. The money, it turned out, went to pay back rent on their a/c.

I had known of Sturgis thru tabloid and news publicity as a mercenary [illegible] a background of petty crimes. He had no steady work, seemingly supported by his wife, Jan.

He made the papers when captured in an insurgent invasion of the D.R. which gave him a certain amount of fame & credibility in the Latino colony.

Apparently Frank had worked for Castro in the mountains and was appointed [illegible] to head Cuba's casinos. Castro soon prohibited casinos + Frank was again jobless. Castro had a sometime mistress in Marita Lorenz. Leaving Castro, she immersed herself in a JFK murder conspiracy and after the deed [illegible] publicly that she

Early in the Bay of Pigs operation Bernie Barker brought Frank Sturgis (nee Fiorini) to my safe house with a defected Cuban who had been chief of Castro's air force. They had overflown Havana and asked for gas money to repeat the leaflet flight. I scrapped together $500 but told them the USG's policy was against it. The money, it turned out, went to pay back rent on their a/c [aircraft].

I had known of Sturgis thru tabloid and news publicity as a mercenary ____ a _____ of petty crimes. He had no steady work, seemingly supported by his wife, Jan.

He made the papers when captured in an insurgent invasion of the D.R. [Dominican Republic] which gave him a certain amount of fame and credibility in the Latino colony.

Apparently Frank had worked for Castro in the mountains and was appointed ____ to head Cuba's casinos.

Castro soon prohibited casinos & Frank was again jobless. Castro had a sometime mistress in Marita Lorenz. Leaving Castro she immersed herself in a JFK murder conspiracy and after the deed ____ publicly that she had ridden in a car w/Sturgis and Hunt, took weapons to Dallas. She kept repeating this lie until Sturgis infuriated, went to her NY apt. with a pistol & tried to break in. Lorenz, ___, called the police and Sturgis was arrested.

Later Sturgis was one of the Watergate conspirators & was arrested in DNC Hqs. Later sentenced to federal prison in Danbury, CT. When his mother died, Frank had no money to attend the funeral w/ 2 federal marshals guarding him. Dr. Manuel Artime gave him the air fares and paid for his mother's casket and funeral expenses.

Frank served 2-3 years at Danbury, where he circulated mainly among Mafia types. He had a ___ ___ and was a slovenly dresser but had an easy ingratiating manner.

After prison, Frank worked in a Miami garage and I lost track of him.

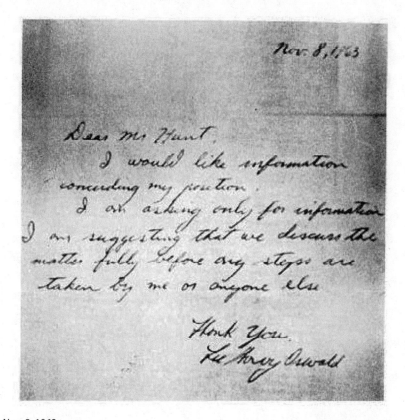

Nov. 8, 1963

Dear Mr. Hunt,
I would like information concerning my position.
I am asking only for information. I am suggesting that we discuss the matter fully before any steps are taken by me or anyone else.

Thank-you,
Lee Harvey Oswald

This note first appeared in the 1970s when it was published by JFK researcher Penn Jones, to whom it had been sent anonymously. There has been speculation, as to whether, the "Mr. Hunt" of the note was either Texan billionaire H.L. Hunt or my father, E. Howard Hunt. But according to a Russian defector and former KGB archivist Vasili Mitrokhin in his book, *The Sword and the Shield: The Mitrokhin Archive and the Secret History of the KGB*, the note is a forgery, created by the KGB to link my father and the CIA to the Kennedy assassination.

My father avoided questions about this note and would only admit that Oswald would have been handled by David Phillips. Phillips was known to be deeply involved in Cuba and anti-Cuba exiles with Antonio Veciana. Phillips was a very close friend and associate of my father.

E. HOWARD HUNT
11337 NE 8TH COURT
MIAMI, FLORIDA 33161
305-895-8415

Dear Saint:

The last I heard of our would-be sponsors was that thet were "preparing papers" and that was a while ago.. It is high time for a "good faith" transfer to be made. Without that I don'¶t want to talk with or negotiate something intangible, This road is one I've traveled before you must forgive me for cynicism:

HOWEVER I F AN AGREEMENT IS TO BE MADE I have two stipulations: Source of the info must not be identdfied, and any all legal charges arising from the enterprise must be paid by sponsors. These two lesspns I leARNED THR Watergate. (Remember the hordes of media folk surroinding our Potomac house???) H said all thatm I look forward to seeing you here. Much love,

Papa

My new dentures are to be ready about the time of the hearing aids + about 3 o/weeks from now

Letter written to me by my father expressing concerns with sponsors Costner and Giammarco.

E. HOWARD HUNT
11337 NE 8TH COURT
MIAMI, FLORIDA 33161
305-895-8415

2/18/04

Dear Saint:

Please let me know exactly what Giammarco/Costner know about my revelations, and what they _don't_ know. This is essential for Snyder and me in negotiating with Costner. This is very important.

Hope all is well at your place.

Love,

Papa

P.S. We'll let you know what (if anything) develops.

Dear Saint,
Please let me know exactly what Giammarco/Costner know about my revelations, and what they <u>don't</u> know. This is essential for Snyder and me in negotiating with Costner. This is very important.
Hope all is well at your place.
Love, Papa

P.S. We'll let you know what (if anything) develops.

from the Partnership. Subject to their availability, each partner shall devote as much time as is reasonably necessary to the interviews and to the creation of the documentary.

REPRESENTATIONS AND ADDITIONAL AGREEMENTS: Each of the partners agrees to sign a depiction release agreement giving to the Partnership the right to use his name and likeness in connection with the Property. Each of the partners agrees to sign additional documents that may reasonably be requested to protect or sell Partnership assets. Each partner represents that he has the right and capacity to enter into this agreement. No consent from the other partners shall be required for a partner to make an assignment of his right to receive income from the Partnership.

RESERVATION OF RIGHTS BY INDIVIDUAL PARTNERS: During his lifetime, HH reserves the right to specify the earliest date that the content of the Property can be released to the general public. KC reserves the right to make "final cuts". KC reserves the right to cancel his obligations to the Partnership if he determines in good faith that the creation of Property would not have sufficient economic merit or if the information furnished for the development of the property is not honest. So that the Partnership business might continue without the participation of KC, if he did decide to cancel his participation, KC would then also offer to assign all of his rights in this Partnership in return for a refund of his capital contributions.

DEATH, INCAPACITY, OR TOTAL DISABILITY of a partner could result in the dissolution of a partnership unless the partners have an agreement concerning these events. Therefore, each partner agrees that such events shall not dissolve this Partnership and it shall continue with the representative(s) or successor(s) in interest of such partner as a Class B Partner. Class B partner shall be entitled to the same rights to distributions but shall have no rights to vote on management matters including the sale or other disposition of the Property.

DISSOLUTION AND TERMINATION OF THE PARTNERSHIP: This partnership shall continue for twenty years and thereafter for the duration of any its copyrights and agreements relating to its Property, unless earlier terminated by the mutual consent of the partners. Upon termination, the business affairs shall be wound up and assets liquidated in an orderly manner.

MISCELLANEOUS: This agreement is the entire agreement of the parties and it cannot be modified except in writing signed by them. This agreement shall be binding upon the parties, their heirs, executors, administrators, and assigns. This agreement shall be governed and controlled by the laws of the State of California. Receive

KC: _____

DG: _____

HH: _____

Signatures of Kevin Costner and David Giammarco on the last page of a three page contract.

UPI

E. Howard Hunt, Jr., the convicted Watergate burglar, straightens his jacket as he arrives in the Senate Caucus Room for the new round of Watergate hearings.

The New York Times/Mike Lien

E. Howard Hunt Jr. testifying before the Watergate committee. At rear are two children, John, 18, and Lisa, 21. Henry Goldman, of law firm representing him, is at left

Some of my collection of news photos about Papa and us during Watergate.

All eyes on their father

St. John and Lisa Hunt watch as their father, admitted Watergate conspirator E. Howard Hunt, testifies before Senate Watergate committee. Hunt, a spy novelist, former CIA agent, and White House consultant, told the committee that former Presidential aide Charles W. Colson approved plans for bugging the Watergate offices of the Democratic National Committee and faking diplomatic cables to discredit the Kennedy Administration. Story on page 1.

Watergate Hearings, Chicago Tribune Sept. 1973

147

Above: Alex Jones shows me the picket fence on the grassy knoll at Dealey Plaza.
Below: Signing autographs during my visit to Dealey Plaza.

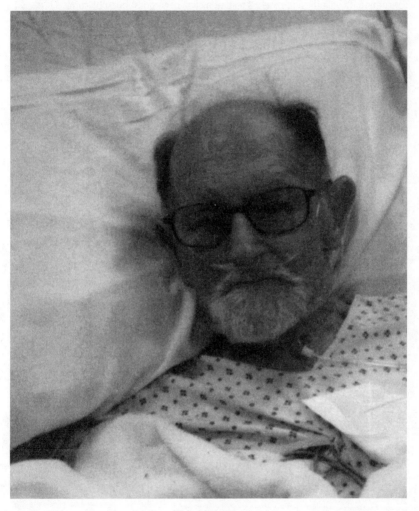

The old warrior.

Even though he confessed he was a "benchwarmer" and named names of folks he said were involved in the JFK assassination, up to his death my father denied this testimony by Marita Lorenz. This deposition was entered into the court record during the course of the retrial of the *Spotlight* libel suit. The full transcript of the deposition does offer quandaries concerning it's validity, and Lorenz's testimony has been questioned by some JFK assassination researchers.

AN EXCERPT FROM *PLAUSIBLE DENIAL*, PP. 291-302.

To present Marita Lorenz's testimony. I arranged for Julia Lee, the wife of Liberty Lobby general counsel Fleming Lee, to study the deposition transcript. At the trial she took the witness chair and answered questions by reading from the transcript. The jury was informed, of course, that the witness was not Lorenz but the testimony was authentic.

The testimony began:

Q: What is your present employment?
A: I do undercover work for an intelligence agency.

Q: Are you permitted to discuss the nature of that work, or where you work?
A: No, I am not.

Q: Is it also true that, as I have stipulated, you do not wish to give your home address?
A: No. I do not.

Q: Have you been employed by the Central Intelligence Agency?
A: Yes.

Q: Are you at liberty to discuss the details of that employment?
A: No.

Q: Have you been employed by the Federal Bureau of Investigation?
A: Yes.

Q: Are you at liberty to discuss that?
A: No.

Q: Have you been employed by the New York Police Department?
A: Yes.

Q: Was that intelligence work?
A: Yes.

Q: Are you at liberty to discuss the details of that work?
A: No.

Q: During 1978, did you appear as a witness before the United States House of Representatives Select Committee on Assassinations?
A: Yes.

Q: Did you appear as a witness after the chief judge of the United States District court of Washington had signed an offer conferring immunity upon you and compelling you to testify?

A: Yes.

My questions and her answers established the foundation for the relationship that existed among Lorenz, Hunt, and Sturgis. I then moved toward the matter at hand.

Q: During and prior to November 1963, did you live in Miami, Florida?

A: Yes, I did.

Q: I want you to understand, if I ask you any question which you are not permitted to answer, you may of course say that, but I will try, based on my previous interview with you, to just ask you questions which you can answer.

A: Yes.

Q: During and before November of 1963, did you work on behalf of the Central Intelligence Agency in the Miami area?

A: Yes.

Q: Did you work with a man named Frank Sturgis, while you were working for the CIA?

A: Yes, I did.

Q: Was that in Miami, during and prior to November 1963?

A: Yes.

Q: What other names, to your knowledge, is Frank Sturgis known by?

A: Frank Fiorini, Hamilton; the last name, Hamilton. F-I-O-R-I-N-I-.

Q: Was Mr. Fiorini or Mr. Sturgis, while you worked with him, also employed by the Central Intelligence Agency?

A: Yes.

Q: During that time were payments made to Mr. Sturgis for the work he was doing for the CIA?

A: Yes.

Q: Did you ever witness anyone make payments to him for the CIA work which you and Mr. Sturgis were both involved in?

A: Yes.

[misc. tidbits deleted...]

It was clear that Lorenz was about to reveal the name of the paymaster and control for Sturgis's secret operations. The courtroom was hushed. Even the miscellaneous spectator background sounds, coughing, clearing of throats, rustling of papers, and moving about came to a sudden, almost eerie, halt.

151

Q: Who did you witness make payments to Mr. Sturgis?

A: A man by the name of Eduardo.

Q: Who is Eduardo?

A: That is his code name; the real name is E. Howard Hunt.

[At this point Hunt began to confer with his attorneys]

Q: Did you know him and meet him during and prior to November 1963?

A: Yes.

We then moved to the events immediately preceding the assassination of President Kennedy.

Q: Did you go on a trip with Mr. Sturgis from Miami during November of 1963?

A: Yes.

Q: Was anyone else present with you when you went on that trip?

A: Yes.

Q: What method of transportation did you use?

A: By car.

Q: Was there one or more cars?

A: There was a follow-up car.

Q: Does that mean two cars?

A: Backup; yes.

Q: What was in the follow-up car, if you know?

A: Weapons.

Q: Without asking you any of the details regarding the activity that you and Mr. Sturgis and Mr. Hunt were involved in, may I ask you if some of that activity was related to the transportation of weapons?

A: Yes.

Q: Did Mr. Hunt pay Mr. Sturgis sums of money for activity related to the transportation of weapons?

A: Yes.

Q: Did Mr. Sturgis tell you where you would be going from Miami, Florida, during November of 1963, prior to the time that you traveled with him in the car?

A: Dallas, Texas.

Q: He told you that?

A: Yes.

Q: Did he tell you the purpose of the trip to Dallas, Texas?

A: No; he said it was confidential.

Q: Did you arrive in Dallas during November of 1963?

A: Yes.

Q: After you arrived in Dallas, did you stay at any accommodations there?

A: Motel.

Q: While you were at that motel, did you meet anyone other than those who were in the party traveling with you from Miami to Dallas?

A: Yes.

Q: Who did you meet?

A: E. Howard Hunt.

Marita Lorenz then provided details about her stay in Dallas.

Q: Was there anyone else who you saw or met other than Mr. Hunt?

A: Excuse me?

Q: Other than those?

A: Jack Ruby.

Q: Tell me the circumstances regarding your seeing E. Howard Hunt in Dallas in November of 1963?

A: There was a prearranged meeting that E. Howard Hunt deliver us sums of money for the so-called operation that I did not know its nature.

Q: Were you told what your role was to be?

A: Just a decoy at the time.

Q: Did you see Mr. Hunt actually deliver money to anyone in the motel room which you were present in?

A: Yes.

Q: To who did you see him deliver the money?

A: He gave an envelope of cash to Frank Fiorini.

Q: When he gave him the envelope, was the cash visible as he had it in the envelope?

A: Yes.

Q: Did you have a chance to see the cash after the envelope was given to Mr. Fiorini?

A: Frank pulled out the money and flipped it and counted it and said "that is enough" and put it in his jacket.

Q: How long did Mr. Hunt remain in the room?

A: About forty-five minutes.

Q: Did anyone else enter the room other than you, Mr. Fiorini, Mr. Hunt, and others who may have been there before Mr. Hunt arrived?

A: No.

Q: Where did you see the person you identified as Jack Ruby?

A: After Eduardo left, a fellow came to the door and it was Jack Ruby, about an hour later, forty-five minutes to an hour later.

Q: When you say Eduardo, who are you referring to?

A: E. Howard Hunt.

The presence of Ruby, the man who had been a hit man for organized crime as early as 1939 in Chicago, and who served as an FBI informant in Dallas since 1959, brought the circle closer.

Q: When did that meeting take place in terms of the hour; was it daytime or nighttime?

A: Early evening.

Q: How soon after that evening meeting took place did you leave Dallas?

A: I left about two hours later; Frank took me to the airport and we went back to Miami.

Q: Now, can you tell us in relationship to the day that President Kennedy was killed, when this meeting took place?

A: The day before.

Q: Is it your testimony that the meeting which you just described with Mr. Hunt making the payment of money to Mr. Sturgis took place on November 21, 1963?

A: Yes.

Q: When was the first time that you met me?

A: In 1977.

Q: On that occasion, did you tell me in words or substance exactly the same thing that you have testified to today?

A: Yes.

The original focus at the first trial by Hunt's lawyer, Ellis Rubin, upon the importance of establishing Hunt's alleged absence from Dallas on November 22, had so skewed the defense that the CIA sought out witnesses and documentary evidence to provide a false alibi for the wrong day.

...Thus Hunt's CIA witnesses, misled as to the implications of the record, focused upon November 22 to the exclusion of the previous day.

...Hunt himself was misled as to his own objective. When I confronted Hunt with the fact that CIA records disclosed that he had taken eleven hours of sick leave in the two-week period ending November 23, 1963, he responded that he was quite sure he had not utilized any of those eleven hours on November 22.

Having decided that he had exculpated himself from the relevant potential accusation, he agreed that it was certainly possible that he had been absent from work on November 21.

...During the Lorenz deposition I inquired about her identification of the man she described as Jack Ruby.

Q: Two days after President Kennedy was assassinated, that is on November 24, 1963, Lee Harvey Oswald, who was arrested and charged with the assassination of President Kennedy and the murder of police officer J.D. Tippit, was killed in Dallas by a man named Jack Ruby?
A: Yes.

Q: On that occasion and subsequent to that time, did you see pictures of Jack Ruby in the newspaper and did you see Jack Ruby on television.
A: Yes, I did.

Q: Is it your testimony that the man who killed Lee Harvey Oswald is, to the best of your ability to identify him, the person who was in the room in the motel in Dallas the night before the president was killed?
A: Yes.

Q: Had you ever seen Jack Ruby before November 21, 1963?
A: No.

Dunne's cross-examination did not succeed in calling into question a single statement that she had made. Indeed, it provided an opportunity for her to fill in a number of details.

...When asked why she had not appeared before the Warren Commission, she testified that she was instructed by her superiors in the CIA not to do so. Dunne persisted.

Q: Is it your testimony today, that today's testimony is consistent with what you said before the House Select Committee?
A: That's right.

Q: When was the first time you met Howard Hunt?
A: 1960, in Miami, Florida.

Q: How was he identified to you?
A: Introduced. Introduced as Eduardo.

Q: How do you spell that?
A: E-D-U-A-R-D-O., Eduardo. E-D-U-A-R-D-O. He was to finance the operations in Miami.

Q: What language did he speak to you in?
A: English and Spanish.

Q: English and Spanish?
A: Yes.

Q: Do you speak Spanish?
A: Yes.

Q: Any other languages?

A: German.

Q: When is it that you became aware that this person you know as Eduardo was E. Howard Hunt?

A: About the same time. Eduardo was the name we were to refer to him as, when discussing things.

Q: Who did you believe he was working for at that time?

A: CIA.

Q: Why?

A: Because we were all at that time CIA members of Operation 40. We had been given instructions from Eduardo and had certain rights and permissions to do things that the average citizen could not do.

When Dunne asked her about her early experiences for the CIA in Cuba she answered:

"I will tell you what is on record. I stole secrets from Cuba. I was trained to kill. Anything else?"

During my interview with Marita prior to the deposition, I had asked for the names of the other persons in the two-car caravan from Miami to Dallas. She was very reluctant to answer that question: "They killed Kennedy. I don't want to be the one to give their names; it's too dangerous." I told her that I would neither pursue the matter then nor inquire of her about their identities at the deposition. I told her that it was possible, however, that Hunt's lawyer might ask that question.

At the deposition, Hunt's lawyer demanded that she provide the name of one more person in the automobile with her. She looked at me, stared at Dunne as if to say, "Well, you asked for this," and responded:

A: The other one was Jerry Patrick ....

Q: Jerry Patrick ... ?

A: Hemming.

Q: Is that, H-E-M-M-I-N-G?

A: Yes.

She added that two Cuban brothers named Novis and a pilot named Pedro Diaz Lanz were also in the caravan.

After the deposition I discussed that question with her. She said, "If Hunt and his friends in the CIA wanted that question answered, or were too dumb or lazy to keep their lawyer from asking it, the responsibility is theirs, not mine."

Dunne wanted to know about the weapons.

Q: Did you see the weapons in the second car?

A: Yes.

Q: What kinds of weapons were there?

A: Handguns and automatics.

Q: Could you identify for me today what kind of guns they were, specifically?

A: Rifles; there were cases of machine guns, rifles, thirty-eights, forty-fives.

Q: Have you been trained in firearms?

A: Yes.

Q: What were the kind of rifles that were there?

A: M-16's, M-1s, shotguns; several.

Q: There were machine guns?

A: Yes.

Q: In your work for the CIA Operation 40, was that one of the major tasks you undertook was to transport guns?

A: Yes.

Q: Was that for the anti-Cuba activities.

A: Yes, it was.

Q: What happened to those guns when you got to Dallas.

A: They were in the car and I presume they took them to the motel the next day, the next night. A lot of things they carried in.

Q: Were did you leave from?

A: From the house in Miami.

Q: Is that a CIA house?

A: A safe house. Yes.

Q: Did everyone meet at the same place?

A: Yes.

Q: Who else was at the house, besides the seven people you identified?

A: This fellow is incarcerated; it is not fair to answer. Another fellow is dead:

Q: Incarcerated where?

A: Out of the country, right now, Venezuela somewhere.

Q: Is his name Bosch?

A: Yes.

Q: What is his first name?

A: Orlando.

Q: Was he one of the anti-Castro Cubans involved in Operation 40?

A: Yes.

Q: Isn't that a matter of public record?

A: Yes.

I broke in to address Dunne: "It's not a matter of public record that he was at the house that day...."

Q: Who was the person at the house that is now deceased?
A: Alexander Rorke, Jr.
Q: Is he a CIA employee?
A: Yes.
Q: What did you do after you got to New York and found out that President Kennedy was just assassinated in Dallas?
A: Talked to the FBI.
Q: You talked to the FBI?
A: Yes.
Q: Voluntarily?
A: They wanted to talk to me about certain things with my child's father and they picked me up and took me to the office.
Q: What day would that have been?
A: A few days after I arrived, after everyone got over the initial shock.
Q: It would be some time in the month of November of 1963?
A: Yes.
Q: In your discussions with the FBI, they inquired about your activities which related to Dallas and this group of seven people that took the car trip?
A: Well, they discussed my associates down there and my relationship with my daughter's father, mostly.
Q: Did they know the names of the people you took the car trip with, from Miami to Dallas?
A: Yes.
Q: Did they ask you about each of those people?
A: Yes.
Q: Did you tell them about the guns and money and about Eduardo?
A: Yes. They asked me about everything, my daughter's father, and I am glad I am back up here away from that.
Q: You told them about Eduardo?
A: Yes.
Q: And the guns?
A: They know about all those associations. They didn't want to go into it. Those were CIA activities, not FBI.

Before the day ended Marita Lorenz explained why she had left Dallas before the assassination:

"I knew that this was different from other jobs. This was not just gun-running. This was big, very big, and I wanted to get out. I told Sturgis I wanted to leave. He said it was a very big operation but that my part was not so dangerous. I was to be a decoy. Before he could go further, I said please let me get out. I want to go back to my baby in Miami.

[...counsel for the prosecution continues - narrating]

Dunne had developed a penchant for not leaving bad enough alone. The testimony of the witness had implicated Hunt and Sturgis in the assassination. Dunne decided to put a fine point to the testimony.

Q: Did you ever talk with Frank Sturgis about it since then?

Lorenz was reluctant to respond directly to the question.

A: We are not on talking terms, Frank and I.
Q: That was not my question. Have you ever talked about it with Frank Sturgis since 1963?
A: Yes.
Q: Did he ever indicate to you that he was involved in the assassination of the President?

A: Yes

Dunne continued to ask questions that Marita Lorenz had requested that I avoid. Due to my commitment to her, I did not make the inquiries, but Dunne rushed in asking questions to which he did not know the answer.

Later Lorenz, prompted by Dunne's questions, explained that when Sturgis sought to recruit her for yet another CIA project, he told her that she had "missed the really big one" in Dallas. He explained, she said, "We killed the President that day. You could have been a part of it – you know, part of history. You should have stayed. It was safe. Everything was covered in advance. No arrests, no real newspaper investigation. It was all covered. Very professional."

Used by permission.
Plausible Denial: Was the CIA Involved in the Assassination of JFK?
Thunder's Mouth Press
© 1991 Mark Lane